D0884026

PATHWAYS TO UNDERSTANDING

OUTDOOR ADVENTURES
IN MEDITATION

by
HAROLD E. KOHN

Author of FEELING LOW?
THROUGH THE VALLEY

Illustrated with Forty-five
Line Drawings by the Author

WM. B. EERDMANS PUBLISHING COMPANY
Grand Rapids, Michigan

PATHWAYS TO UNDERSTANDING
Copyrighted 1958, by
Harold E. Kohn

LIBRARY OF CONGRESS CATALOG CARD NUMBER: 58-7573

PRINTED IN THE UNITED STATES OF AMERICA

Dedication

HIS BOOK IS AFFECTION-
ATELY DEDICATED to
Carolyn, my beloved
daughter and ideal com-
panion, whose presence is
as refreshing as a balsam-
scented breath of the out-
of-doors.

Preface

For more than four years these brief essays, all dealing with problems of everyday life and how they can be handled victoriously, have appeared in the local press. Each article has been presented in parable form, having as its background some experience the author has enjoyed with nature while sauntering over the wild acres of Hidden Brook, his woodland retreat, or while visiting some lakeside haunts at Wide Sky Harbor where he lives with his family, or occasionally while simply looking contemplatively from his study window over the broad shimmering expanse of Lake Charlevoix. Two earlier books of these essays have been published, *Feeling Low?* and *Through the Valley.* The present volume was prepared to supplement and complement the first two.

The purpose of this book is to discuss informally and intimately with the reader some observations I have made in nature that may serve as clues to what we are, the attitudes we should take toward life and its Creator, and how we might best look upon life's mysteries.

The parable form of discussion is used for the reasons Jesus employed it — because of a natural correspondence between the things of earth and the things of heaven, because we most easily grasp an invisible truth when it has a visible handle, and because of the age-old delight all humans find in stories. An old Scottish lady once exclaimed to Dr. Thomas Guthrie, "The parts of the Bible I like best are the *likes!*" Most of us could agree. We cherish those passages of Scripture that begin, "The kingdom of heaven is like . . . ." For twenty centuries the world has listened to the familiar comparisons: "The kingdom of heaven is like a net which was thrown into the sea and gathered fish of every kind"; "The kingdom of heaven is like a treasure hidden in a field"; "The kingdom of heaven is like a grain of mustard seed." When the Master Teacher sought to illumine truth, He often lighted it with some comparison with an object already familiar to His listeners. Mark's Gospel says of His teaching by the seaside one day, "With many . . . parables he spoke the word to them, as they were able to hear it; he did not speak to them without a parable." The parable was Jesus' favorite method of making spoken truth plain, real, and memorable. His method has been used here for the same reasons.

For whatever good is found in these pages thanks are due to Hidden Brook and to Wide Sky Harbor, places of peace, inspiration, and growing wonder, and to the multitude of wild things that grow, scamper, swim, and fly there.

Special acknowledgment is given to the congregation of the First Congregational Church of Charlevoix, a splendid people who most certainly inspire their minister fully as much as he ever can hope to inspire them and who constantly encourage this writing ministry.

I am indebted also to the Reverend A. R. Gold, my friend and colleague in the ministry, who has been a source of much assurance and whose enthusiastic cooperation in our common service to the church has been most heartening.

Many Northeners who have come to me in distress will recognize in these pages some of the problems they have brought to me and certain of the principles for triumphant living we have discussed by the fireside at Wide Sky Harbor. To these lonely, guilt-laden, perplexed, or bereaved people I express warm thanks. I am grateful, too, for the many readers of my column and earlier books who have written me so intimately of their deepest hurts, highest joys, and biggest questions. These searchers for insight and fulfillment have drawn out, as well as taken in, the messages contained in this book.

Most of these chapters appeared first in *The Charlevoix Courier,* published weekly at Charlevoix, Michigan, and I express deep appreciation for many courtesies extended to me by the editor, Harold Totten, and his staff.

The article entitled "The Best Things Cannot Be Hurried" appeared in condensed form in *The Reader's Digest* for December, 1956, and in fourteen of the International Editions of that publication, and I express my thanks to Editors DeWitt

Wallace and Lila Acheson Wallace for permission to print the complete article in these pages.

Most of all, I am everlastingly grateful to my wife, Marian, and daughter, Carolyn, who provide a happy atmosphere at home and who make returning homeward as exciting and enjoyable as stepping into the world of nature.

Now that we have been properly introduced, come along with me and let us wander over some pathways of understanding.

HAROLD E. KOHN

Wide Sky Harbor
Charlevoix, Michigan
February, 1958

9

CONTENTS

11

Pathways to Understanding

1

Collectors

While sauntering about in woods and fields, an alert observer is impressed with the collecting habits of Nature's children. A fox squirrel races to the ground from a high oak limb where he has picked a ripe acorn. Swiftly he digs a small hole, caches the nut near others he has previously hidden, and scampers up the oak tree's bole again to search for more provender against days of winter scarcity. Sometimes a small collection of acorns is forgotten by its planter, and in years to come oak trees will stand there, tall, leafy testimonies to the squirrel's absent-mindedness.

Occasionally a "mushroom tree" is seen in a forest or field, with mushrooms showing in every crotch where branches meet. These are usually the hoarding of red squirrels, avid lovers of mushrooms. They nibble on a few of these fungi as soon as they find them. But many they gather and set aside for future use.

Butcher birds, also known as shrikes, collect and impale other birds and small rodents on thorns or barbed wire fences. When hunger gnaws at their vitals they return to their larder for a taste of their collection.

The collecting habit is prevalent among human beings, too. The first farmers were collectors. They ranged the hillsides, valleys and forests, seeking their favorite herbs and roots. Having observed that food plants grew more plentifully and more luxuriantly under certain conditions — as in refuse dumps where seeds and pits were thrown — they returned repeatedly to such favorable places to gather their choicest plants. In our times civilized man spares himself the bother and effort of collecting his vegetable food from over a vast expanse by concentrating

his crops on farms and in gardens. There he separates them into types — a certain plot for grains, another tract for potatoes, and still other areas for cabbages, beets, lettuce and sundry other foods. Nevertheless, man is still a collector, and when harvest time arrives he goes about gathering what the warm sun, the soft rains, and the fertile soil have grown.

The human propensity for collecting is evidenced by man's hobbies. Children and grownups alike gather stamps, coins, match-covers, and figurines. Some men have cabinets filled with old guns. The wealthy collect original paintings of the old masters. "Bobby-soxers" hoard the autographs of their favorite crooners, and those who can afford them may purchase the signatures and letters of great men and women of history.

A New York woman collects cats' whiskers and owns over five hundred specimens. A modern Casanova of St. Paul, Minnesota, has confessed to collecting locks of hair from every girl he kisses. He pastes the tresses on sheets of paper, labeling them with date, place, the girl's name, and noting his impressions at the moment of impact! The extent of his collection has reached three hundred locks. All known colors of human hair are included.

Some people collect faults, as the St. Paul man does kisses. They make mental notes of what is wrong with every person they meet. More often than not, this hobby arises from their feelings of inadequacy and unworthiness. It is as if their subconscious mind were saying, "I'm not much good. So what? Nobody else is worth much either if you take a good look at him. Everybody I meet has something wrong with him. I guess I'm as good as the next fellow."

A noted soprano gave a remarkable concert one night — perfect in every respect except one. Aiming for an unusually high note, she "flatted." When a certain crowd got together for a post-concert party, the only thing they could talk about was that one flat note. The soprano had sung thousands of notes to perfection. But the fault-collectors weren't interested in them. Perfect notes wouldn't do. For their collection of mistakes they needed a flat.

Then there are the slight-collectors. Talk to them for a while and they will wax enthusiastic about their hobby. With relish they will name their latest additions of indignities suffered, the humiliations they have undergone, the snubs they have acquired. Some of their slights are really beautiful to behold, polished to gem-like perfection from much handling and exquisite care.

The most admirable people, as well as the most insufferable, are collectors. Some whom I know have assembled an impressive array of glorious memories. Involve them in conversation and within a few moments you are treated to a spread of radiant recollections of golden moments they have experienced.

One elderly woman collects moments of gratitude for favors, some received from God and others from dear ones on earth. Her theme song is an old hymn I've heard her sing innumerable times while she worked about her kitchen, her laundry room, and her garden:

> Count your blessings,
>   Name them one by one.
> Count your many blessings,
>   See what God has done.

Everyone is a collector, owning an accumulation of evil, of the mediocre, or the best. You are a collector too. What do you save and cherish?

2

Living with Limitations

What a queer world this would become if suddenly the limitations of size and time were removed from everything. Then ants would grow larger than cows, and violets and wild strawberries would tower higher than houses. I've thought of this while reflecting upon the vast variety of things that live and grow at our woodland retreat. Most living things are about the same size, well-nigh microscopic, at the time of their conception. But how different they are upon reaching maturity!

Although the germ cell that initiates a fox squirrel's life is almost identically the size of the cell from which a whitetail deer develops, no mature squirrel at Hidden Brook or in North America or in the entire world ever attains the size of our Michigan deer. Why?

The seedlings of giant Pacific Coast sequoia trees were once no larger than our infant spruces now growing on the brook bank, but no Hidden Brook spruce will ever reach the 300-foot height or the 30-foot diameter or the 4000-year age of one giant redwood in the Caleveras Grove of California. Why?

Living things of every kind seem to have built-in limitations. Sometimes it is a limitation of size, a physiological optimum, so that no mouse, no matter how healthy or well fed, ever achieves the enormous proportions of an elephant. In other cases the limitation is a kind of life-tether, a time boundary, beyond which the creature cannot reach. Thus a well-fed brook trout will continue to grow as long as it lives, but it is an exceedingly rare trout that reaches the age of fifteen years.

Man, too, is a limited creature. Nature sets boundaries to what he can be and do. Man cannot greatly alter his height. A man eight feet tall is a freak, and a man of fifteen-foot stature has never been known. Modern medicine has extended our

life expectancy, but it is still limited and always will be. Many a tortoise (perhaps the longest-lived animal) lives to be more than two hundred and fifty years of age, but seldom does a human being, and no man has achieved the age of an ancient cypress tree, The Big Tree of Tule, near Mexico City. Biologists estimate its age to be over five thousand years.

One of life's most important discoveries is that of finding our possibilities, what we can do with ourselves and with the opportunities for good that are presented to us. Another significant insight all of us need is the revelation of our limitations. Said the Chinese philosopher, Lin Yutang, "Sometimes it is more important to know what one *cannot* do, than it is to know what one can do."

When we have limitations and act as if we have none, we are like a person with fifty dollars in savings who spends like a lavish millionaire. We are soon bankrupt. The social climber who tries to be all things to all people so as to please them and gain favor with them is headed for insolvency of character. She can be but one person and still maintain integrity. When she ignores that limitation her character is ruined. She loses her real self amidst the pretensions.

Basically, I suppose, much of the sin of ignoring our limitations is founded upon the folly of playing God. We behave as if we were the Infinite, Almighty, All-Knowing.

Some play God by trying to reform the entire world as if the Creator, upon viewing His mismanaged universe, had in shame abdicated His throne, and they were appointed to succeed Him and remedy the botched-up job. With smug, critical, and confident mien they start with human beings God blundered in making. They are nosy, attempting to pry into all their neighbors' affairs and making snap judgments about the morals and motives of others, as if they were God and could see all, know all, and stand in lofty judgment upon all human activity. They are the neighborhood busy-bodies, the holier-than-thou critics. Goodness knows there is enough evil in the world that needs righting, and everyone should assist in combating it. But these people who play God seldom will assume responsibility for *righting* wrong. They want merely to be all-knowing without paying the price of being redemptive and helping to change people and alter circumstances.

Others play God by assuming too much responsibility — unlimited responsibility — for the conditions of the world and everyone in it. They seem unable to see where their accountabilities end. They continue to treat their children as infants long after the youngsters should be responsible for themselves. They are the doting mothers and dads who make interfering, meddling parents-in-law because they insist upon managing a daughter's or son's home life after the child is married. They tell their grown children what kind of house to buy. They try to direct their investments. They boss the grandchildren. Spreading their misdirected and exaggerated feelings of responsibility still further, they join too many committees, attend too many benefit luncheons, get elected to positions in too many societies and clubs, and then they are not content to be a cooperating part of the organization. They must direct it. Their plan of action is the only one that can be adopted or certain disaster will confront the group. Such people are playing God, assuming the direction of virtually the whole universe. And since the universe is not built upon their wishes and will not be governed by their whims, they are constantly upset, irritated, and disappointed. Because they have faith in none other than their own designs and plans, they are constantly anxious and worried since the universe is run on a scheme concerning which they were never consulted.

Whenever we squander our time as if it were unlimited, we are playing the part of the Eternal.

Whenever we are bigoted in our opinions or maliciously assume that we know all a person's motives and intentions and therefore have a right to judge him lightly, we are playing the part of the Omniscient.

Whenever we try to bring everyone under our control and assume direction of all the activities in which we are engaged with others, and whenever we worry, fret, and fume about a multiplicity of events that stretch from our doorstep to Timbuctoo, as if the universe would go to smash if we were not constantly awake and at the helm, we are playing the part of the Omnipotent.

The world's real servants are people with a balanced insight, people who know what they can do and what must be done, and they do it.

But just as important, they have a peace-bestowing humility, knowing what they cannot do. And what they cannot do they leave in the capable hands of One who can.

3

When the Bird Walks

A friend who just arrived in Michigan's Northland from Ohio says that spring is really on its way to us. As she passed through southern Michigan she heard a bobwhite sing. That was proof, she felt, that Nature is awakening from a long winter's nap.

The call-notes of the bobwhite, the song of the first robin, the trooping of the warblers as they steadily move still farther northward, are welcome sounds and sights. To one who loves Nature the return of the birds is like the sudden glad reappearance of friends whose company we have greatly missed.

What is a bird? If you were to define a bird to a blind person who had never seen one, doubtlessly you would list its wings among its outstanding characteristics. You would describe its capacity for flight. Yet for how brief a time out of a twenty-four-hour day most birds stay on the wing! The bobwhite quail, the robin, the wren, the ruffed grouse, the bluebird — nearly all our most familiar and best-loved birds — spend more time with wings folded than they do in flight. Yet, as some ancient seer has said, "Even when the bird walks we see that he has wings."

We human beings are bird-like in one respect at least. Our capacity for flight is used only on rare occasions. Faith rarely is summoned to take wings and soar. Infrequently are we called upon to exercise extreme courage. Utmost patience and lavish forgiveness are uncommonly needed. Most of the time our souls are grounded, walking rather than flying. Yet when a good soul walks we see that he has wings.

We may be no high-flying orators, but are there wings in our ordinary conversation? Does our discourse with others lift them? We may think we could do tremendous good if we were wealthy, possessing millions. We would build orphanages, support the aged, provide for medical missions. With millions we would

25

do wonders. But what are we doing with the little we have? Are we helping to the extent of our present ability?

"If I were a world leader, I would bring peace to the world," we say to ourselves. But are we living at peace with our neighbors? Do we have any unsolved hostile relationships with acquaintances?

In the shelter of the entrance to an empty store building a little old wizened magazine vendor had set up his shop. Scattered about on a small table was his merchandise. Colorful booklets were displayed against a velvet background stretched over a clumsily constructed rack. Above the rack was a worn and weathered sign bearing the inscription:

HOW TO SUCCEED

READ YOUR OWN HOROSCOPE

As the pitiful little fellow tended to his negligible business, any passer-by was apt to smile at the pathetic incongruity plainly present there. Here was a man whose business was a total failure offering the world advice on "how to succeed."

How often we feel we could change the world, if the opportunity were given to us. But have we improved our homes? Is our community better because we live here?

The grace of God is more than the power to soar on rare occasions. It is the capacity to walk, through joys and disappointments, applause and criticism, successes and failures, and still to let the world see that we have wings.

4

We Belong to Each Other

Living things belong to each other. None of them attempt to "go it alone." The grass that binds the soil together on the brook bank belongs to the cow that eats it and to the turtle whose stream-home the grass protects from erosion-produced muddiness. Spruces and hemlocks, balsam and birches rimming the meadow draw upon the moisture of the soil, as do the abundant grasses, and bask in the same sun. Air breathers drink in the same oxygen. Fishes share the same stream with ducks and with each other.

When an animal eats a plant, as when a cow eats grass, the plant actually becomes animal. Plant material, when digested, is carried by the blood stream to every cell of the animal and there is built into animal flesh. In turn, carbon dioxide, an animal waste, is breathed out into the atmosphere and is then' absorbed by vegetation which uses it in building plant cells. The varieties of beings in a Northland wildlife community would be beyond calculation, but they all fit into a single design. They belong to each other.

Aldo Leopold, the late great natural scientist, once studied the interrelationships of rabbits, lady-slippers, deer, and grouse in the woods of his beloved Wisconsin. He found rabbits especially abundant between the years of 1932 and 1935. They nibbled down the little bog-birch, a small bush of which they are fond. This hurt the deer and grouse population, for starving deer browse on the tips of these bushes, and sharptail grouse count bog-birch buds among their staple foods. Moreover, the abundance of rabbits affected the lady-slipper population, but in a far different way. When the rabbits ate bog-birches which had shaded the forest floor, more sunlight reached the small plant-life there. Sunlight was needed by lady-slippers, which flourished under the new conditions.

When in the years 1936 and 1937 the rabbit population suddenly fell off, bog-birches made a quick come-back. Grouse and deer then benefited from larger amounts of emergency provender. But lady-slippers, hidden by bog-birches from the sun, languished and failed. Rabbits, lady-slippers, bog-birches, deer, and sharp-tailed grouse belong to each other. All are part of the same parcel of life.

Self-sufficiency is a myth. There is no such thing as a completely self-sufficient person. We are linked to all other forms of life, to all forms of non-living things, to each other. You and I, the whirling earth and its inhabitants, the beneficent sun and the most distant stars belong to one cosmic family. We are all made of the same star dust and earth dust. We share a composition of the same basic chemicals. We are part of each other and belong to one another.

A realization of this principle of interrelatedness ought to do something for us. For one thing, it should free us from our foolish treatment of cooperation as some remote ideal to be achieved and make us aware that it is a fact which already confronts us. We already cooperate (which means that we operate together). We can't help it, since none is self-sufficient. We need only to do it better, much better! To tell people they ought to cooperate is like telling them they ought to eat. They already eat. They will always eat, or die. But millions should be taught about proper nutrition and sound eating practices. In a similar way, people ought not be told that it would be ideal if they learned to cooperate. Instead, the cooperation in which we are already the involuntary participants should become clear to us. The unconscious cooperation should become conscious and appreciated. The kinds of cooperation should be multiplied and broadened and strengthened until our understanding of our oneness is deepened and our obedience to the rule of living for the welfare of the entire human family becomes a basic objective of our lives.

Furthermore, being alive to the fact that we belong to each other should make us more grateful for each other and less critical of one another. Why be irritated because others vary from us in their interests, talents, and insights? If we were all alike, life would lose much of its richness. There could be no new ideas, because new ideas come to us from others, and if we were all alike in our thinking, every idea you ever heard expressed would be one you had thought of before. There could be no exchange of services, because, if everyone were like you, he could do nothing better than you could do it yourself, and if we all felt alike no one would perform a service for you that you were reluctant to carry out. Having feelings exactly like your own, he would be reluctant! An employer could find no employees because everyone would want to be employers. There could be no colleges or universities, because no one would want to do the janitor work or maintain the buildings or be students. Everyone would want to be an honored professor or he would have nothing to do with the school. No one on top of the heap can intelligently look down his nose on those at the bottom. The big apples on top of the basket are there only because there are a lot of little ones under them holding them up there. People on top of the management basket in business, the learning basket in education, the upper crust in society need to remember that. The little apples are keeping them up there.

This consciousness of our interdependence is distinctive of great men. They know their achievements are not solo performances, but done in concert with others, many of whom are unknown to them. Albert Einstein spoke of his indebtedness to others in this fashion: "Many times a day I realize how much my own outer and inner life is built upon the labors of my fellowmen, both living and dead, and how earnestly I must exert myself in order to give in return as much as I have received."

Some years ago before great pipe organs were operated with the aid of electricity, a noted organist was playing before an enthusiastic audience. A small boy labored hard behind a screen, pumping the organ for all he was worth. During the intermission the youngster, flushed with pride, said to the famous musician, "Aren't we wonderful?" "Who's we?" barked the organist as he stomped off to play the second half of his program. As he sat down to the organ console, the musician stroked the keys, but not a note came forth. Alarmed, he struck the keyboard savagely, and still no sound. At last a small voice came from behind the organ screen, "Now, who's we?"

Who are "we" anyway? As a person matures his "we" concept grows until "we" embraces all the people of the world, the great and the unknown, the old and the young, the rich and the poor, of every color and of all nations. And when "we" takes in every living thing, a person has finally found himself at home in the world.

5

The Meaning of Greatness

While watching wild animals one is bound to admire their quick interest in anything unusual that happens near them.

The smell and sight of a curling wisp of smoke has been known to draw whitetail deer through the woods to see what is going on. Antelope of our western plains are so insatiably curious that old-time hunters brought them into shooting range by hiding behind sagebrush and waving a white handkerchief. Antelope would approach the sage while trying to puzzle out what that fluttering whiteness was, and the hunter would have his advantageous shot.

Hang the bright and shining lid of a tin can from a low limb in the north woods and visit it a few days later. Chances are you will find there the tracks of a curious raccoon which has peered up at it and has walked on his hind legs beneath it, trying to reach it. Many a trapper uses this trick to catch raccoons, simply suspending a shining object over a hidden trap. A wild creature's interest in the world around him and his frequent forgetfulness of the danger he may be in is a thought-provoking trait.

An animal's comparative lack of self-interest is at the same time one of its severest limitations and its chief charm. While the animal psychologists, who make a lifetime study of animal behavior, admit they have found no satisfactory way of telling what other creatures "think" about, still it is their conclusion that an animal gives little thought to himself.

A man looks into a mirror and, with its aid, combs his hair. While watching herself in a mirror a woman applies powder and rouge or lipstick. Both know they see themselves in that mirror. But when a monkey peers into a mirror he thinks he sees another monkey, and begins looking behind the glass in further search of him. Man is the only creature that makes

33

and uses mirrors for seeing himself, or keeps diaries of his own performances, or writes autobiographies, or develops a science of introspection such as psychology. Man is the animal with the most self-interest.

A badly limited self-awareness has its compensations. If a monkey lacks sufficient self-interest to recognize itself in a mirror, neither can it indulge in neurotic self-pity, feeling unappreciated or persecuted, or the victim of cruel fate. If a whitetail buck deer cannot paw out a diary record on a tablet of freshly fallen snow or on a scratch pad of sandy beach, neither can he feel that he deserves more attention than a hard-hearted world gives him. If a snowshoe rabbit cannot self-consciously play the hero, neither will he take the role of a martyr, making wild claims of how much he has sacrificed for his family and friends. If a chickadee cannot probe into its own inner life and see the good that is there, neither can it deceive itself, pretending that it has virtues that are actually non-existent, as can a human mother who "loves" her son so much that she disapproves of every girl he dates and prevents his marrying and leaving home. If a creature cannot be credited with self-awareness, neither can it be blamed for self-deception.

One of the grandest things about man is his capacity to *have* self-interest without constantly *using* it. Man's greatness often lies in putting aside his self-awareness for a while and being self-forgetful. The record of good done in the world has been made largely by men and women whose attention was not on themselves so much as on their ideals, their purpose, their mission. Their interests were absorbed by the significance of what they were doing, and they, themselves, were great without knowing it.

The process of growing up mentally and spiritually is, in part, one of enlarging the scope of our attention so that we become more and more aware of the importance of things and people and meanings other than ourselves. Before children acquire the restraints of modesty and learn to suppress expressing their need for attention, appreciation, affection, and applause, they freely ask, "Now watch me, Daddy," as they jump off the front porch, or, "See what I can do, Mommy?" as they ride their tricycle with hands off the handlebars. Some people are fixated at that stage of development, throughout life continually pleading, "Now watch me!"

As we mature in mind and spirit our self-awareness is not expressed in such self-absorption. We are conscious that other things have happened besides *my* birth, that other matters count besides *me*, that there are other events that bear watching besides *my* own performances and that others have problems as severe as *my* own.

One would naturally think the severely handicapped would be most self-conscious of all. Lameness, deafness, blindness, abject poverty or any number of limitations are apt to make one feel "different" from others, set-off, and unusually preoccupied with self. But, oddly, there are among the handicapped those who seem never so much cognizant of their own burden as they are of the problems of others. One kindly woman made this discovery at a circus. She sponsored a trip for a group of handicapped children to a circus performance at Madison Square Gardens in New York. Some were blind. Some were deaf. Others were mute. On their way home one little blind boy exclaimed to the woman, "I sure felt sorry for those deaf boys and girls today!" "Why?" asked the woman. "Why did you feel sorry for those deaf children?" "Because," answered the lad, "they couldn't hear the band. They couldn't hear the lion's big roar, or the crowd clapping for the clowns. They couldn't even hear the elephants clump-clumping by."

A few years ago the *Evening Times* of Little Falls, New York, carried the story of a 13-year-old Paines Hollow boy who heard an appeal being made at Mohawk Central School for contributions to Santa Claus Anonymous, which provided Christmas gifts for the less fortunate children of the school district. The youngster saved all his pennies. On the Friday before Christmas vacation he counted 15 cents he had scrimped and saved for Santa Claus Anonymous. He had planned to turn it in at school that day, but a blizzard heaped the roads with snow and the school buses didn't run, and he was stranded miles from school. After some thought the boy started off from home and struggled through deep drifts, finally arriving at the school where he found Principal Harold Rankin.

When the boy offered his 15 cents, Mr. Rankin awkwardly accepted it with serious misgivings and while swallowing hard.

But his embarrassment was understandable. The lad was one of the youngsters on the list to receive a gift from Santa Claus Anonymous.

Wherever found, in little child or national hero, greatness is self-forgetfulness.

6

Reflected Glory

These spring nights, while the chill air throbs with calls of migrating birds, I have been watching the moon shine over Lake Charlevoix. Hanging low in the sky, this near neighbor to our earth seems for a time to be impaled upon a tall, lonely pine. Then it pulls free and rises in the wide freedom of the sky, silhouetting a flight of birds bound northward toward summer nesting grounds. A silent silver rain of moonlight ripples the lake's broad expanse, giving waves a moister look than is their wont.

This ball of gentle light climbing about the night sky, honored by poets and theme of lovers' songs, is neither so big nor so incandescent as it appears to be. Although the full moon, because of its nearness to us, appears to be as large as the sun, actually it would take about four hundred moons, side by side, to make a heavenly body the diameter of the sun. We would not notice the moon at all if the light of the sun did not strike it, because, say the astronomers, the moon has no light of its own, but simply reflects the radiance of the hidden sun.

People who feel inferior, who have no genius and who generate no inner light of their own, often despair of being of any account in the world. But even those who have the least inner splendor can give to the world such a light as the moon offers, a reflected glory. Not everyone can be great, but we all know of some shining person whose life has illuminated his time. Through biography we can bask in his courage and faith, sense the glow of his integrity, allow our dark minds to be illumined by his thoughts, and catch the blaze of his bigness of heart. Having caught another's effulgence, we can mirror it as the moon does the sun.

Christ-likeness does not mean duplicating Christ's life. It consists rather in exposing heart and mind to Him and then

reflecting His splendid spirit upon the world. Godliness is the gentle light a person lets fall upon his time after first receiving it from fellowship with the Eternal.

We are not suns, but moons. We cannot generate goodness, but all can send forth a reflected glory.

7

Dare to Be Yourself

Brushing the teeth nightly before going to bed is a widespread practice and a good one. A rarer habit and even better is that of giving the mind a good scrubbing every night before retiring, scouring away the day's accumulation of grime.

One of the best brain-brushes I know of is starlight. It is especially effective if used on a crisp, cold wintry night when there is not a fleck of cloud in the sky, when the air is calm and smoke rises easily and hardly ruffled from the fireplace chimney, and when the watcher stands off apart from human habitation, detached, undisturbed, solitary. Then starlight rinses disorder from a jumbled mind, reminding one of the perfect system of the celestial arrangement where entire constellations can dash through the heavens at incomprehensible and varying velocities and in different directions, yet with no collision, no chaos. Such contemplation straightens an untidy mind and cleanses it of all clutter.

Again, starlight wipes away our absorption with the trivial. How small and insignificant we feel and how petty some anxieties, some slights and grievances seem when compared to the spaces that separate the stars. Look up. Consider that the distances between even the closest, most companionable luminaries are somewhat proportionate to the distance between the weathervanes on two church steeples — one located in San Francisco and the other in Tokyo. And the chances of two near stars colliding would be about the same as those weathervanes have of clashing. The consciousness of such enormity and boundlessness scrubs away preoccupation with trivialities and readies a place for great thoughts.

One of the chief benefits derived from frequent star baths is a cleansing of the mind from monotony and sameness. The night sky is full of variety. Every star is an individual with its own position on any given night, its own magnitude, its own hue. Alcor and Megrez of the Big Dipper have their own characteristics and could not be mistaken for Polaris. Orange-colored Arcturus, sixth brightest star in the sky and 25 million miles in diameter, could never be confused with brilliant, bluish-white Vega. There is but one super-giant Betelgeuse, but one Castor, only one Pollux. And when one gets to know the night sky well, the stars are no longer a mass of indistinguishable lights. They are distant but cordial friends, each one known for its own singular charm.

In these days of increasing conformity I find much relief under the starlit heavens where every star has its own degree of luminosity and every planet reflects light with its own intensity. There is in the heavens the same sort of diversity that exists amidst the flowers of earth, where orchids make no attempt to look like roses, nor do roses seek to smell like dahlias. Each wafts its own perfume.

One of the basic evils of our times is our gradual relinquishing of individuality. It can be found almost anywhere in modern society. We are becoming increasingly imitative, fearful of being "different."

David Riesman, one of our generation's profoundly analytical thinkers, has written a book entitled *The Lonely Crowd,* in which he makes close examination of present American character. This author says that before World War I the typical American lived as if he were given balance and stability by some inner gyroscope of motive, ambition, and conviction. But something has happened. The average American seeks now to "fit in," "to find out what others expect of him and then to do it." He is no longer guided from within, but from without. He conforms.

Not long ago one of our most widely circulated magazines published an article concerning the role of the wives of corporation executives. The writer showed profound concern because in many corporations whether or not a man gets a promotion depends a great deal upon whether his wife fits into "the pattern." The wife of the prospective office-holder is eyed as carefully and as zealously as if she were a commodity the firm were buying. She must not be too intelligent. She must move easily in social circles, and she must be very adaptable. Above all, she must not be outstandingly good at anything, not conspicuous. She must not be herself at her worst, but neither can she be herself at her best. She must be what those of her husband's circle expect her to be. She must conform.

Some sociologists declare that conformity to standards of their gang pulls young people into juvenile delinquency that ranges from looseness in sex morals to crimes punishable by death. Too many youngsters have antennae-type minds that are constantly feeling out the group to see what is accepted and what pleases the majority. Whatever it is, they will do it. They do not dare to be different.

Perhaps we can sense the terror and tragedy of conformity most clearly by seeing that by compelling conformity Mussolini's fascism won Italy, Hitlerism took over Germany, and the Communists have seized much of Europe. Wherever an absolute dictator is in control, one can never know when hobnailed boots will kick in a door and summon one to conformity or death. On the other hand, one of the glories of democracy is that it guarantees a maximum of opportunity for disagreement, non-conformity, and individuality.

One of the splendors of greatness is that one heroic person is not a carbon copy of any other. Moses and Jeremiah were both men of enormous spiritual stature. But they were not alike. Peter and Paul were of immense influence on early Christianity, but each in his own way.

One George Washington as President of the United States was momentous for America. But fifteen or thirty successive George Washingtons would not have brought our country to her present greatness. He was the man for that hour, but he himself refused a third term, knowing he was not the man for *every* hour.

Aside from Christ, Abraham Lincoln is my favorite historical personage. Chief among his attributes was his uniqueness. He was different. Never before was there a man like him. Never again will there be a man cut from the same pattern. That fact is not one to be lamented. It is part of Lincoln's splendor that he was and is inimitable. Lincoln's most ardent admirers glory in the knowledge that he can never be duplicated.

Even Christ did not ask that His followers become exact copies of Him. They were to live by His principles and by

His spirit and with His help, but each in his own place with his own gifts and in his own way.

The moon is a sublime sky lantern. But a hundred moons in the sky, the same size and the same shape, would sicken the eye. Stars are splendid. But if all the stars were of the same size and shone with the same intensity and hue, the night sky could not be nearly so beautiful.

Nature never repeats herself, never exactly imitates her past performance.

A long and contemplative look at the stars suggests to a thoughtful person the need of shining in his own place, at his own magnitude, and with his own hue.

8

What Do You See?

Most of us are nearly blind. Even those whose eyes test 20-20 have limited vision. We don't see well.

Give yourself a simple test and see how well you do:

Without looking at the person nearest to you, describe his or her clothing (in polite, inoffensive language, of course!). What color shirt and trousers and tie, or dress, or blouse and skirt, is the person wearing?

You have seen your neighbor's car dozens of times. What kind of ornament decorates the radiator? What color are the seat covers? What is the first number on the license plate? The last number?

What color eyes does your grocer have? Your milkman? The paper boy? Your service station attendant?

Who ushered at your church last Sunday? Was the last person you saw passing your home old or young, a man or a woman?

Do you say, "I saw, but I forgot"? That won't do — not if we apply the deeper meaning of seeing. There is a sort of seeing that is shallow, in which things pass before our "line of vision," but leave no impression upon the mind. Those things can hardly be forgotten because they never registered, were never remembered — even for a moment. Then, again, some seeing is meaningful because it is penetrating and attentive — like the first breath-taking glimpse of your first-born child, or the way the wife looked when you announced that at last you had the down payment for your first home, or better yet, the way she looked when you could first call her "Mrs." Or, do you remember the first tremulous steps your baby took, or the look on his face on his first Christmas, or the doctor's expression when,

after the fever broke, he said, "Your child will be all right now in a few days"? These things you saw and remembered because they *interested* you. They "counted" with you.

As evening falls, a man stands on a marsh's edge where ducks swim about, family style. Man and duck have eyes constructed very much alike, with iris, cornea, pupil, lens, retina, and optic nerve. But what do they really see?

The duck will notice those things in which ducks have a vital interest — an insect upon the water's surface, or a predaceous hawk circling high in the heavens, hungry for warm duck flesh. And the man will hold and mark those things that interest him, and the wider his range of interests, the broader and richer his mind, the more he will observe. If he is a meat-hungry poacher with a gun, he will see ducks as meat. If he is an engineer, he will see ducks as examples of propulsion, their paddles efficiently placed near the rear of their bodies to give them more "push," as a marine motor is housed astern. But if the man has an expansive, inclusive mind, he sees more than duck meat and an example of naval engineering. He sees more than his own practical interests. He is attentive to swimming ducks, drowning insects, waving rushes, evening mists dimming the sunset and enshrouding the shining waters. The "practical man" has only partial vision, for he sees only what he came to see, and what his past experience compels him to notice. The growing soul sees these things and more, too. He looks for the new, the thus-far-unnoticed, the wholesomely different, and he stuffs it into an already full mind. And the mind stretches to a greater magnitude. This kind of appreciative seeing always results in greater minds and bigger men.

How about it now? What do you see? Just what you expected and hoped to see? Concerning your church, are only those sermons "good" which reinforce your own thinking, or are you glad when your minister offers you new insight and a point of view which collides with your established convictions? And, of course, there are our neighbors to be seen. Does it please us to say of those we know, "What did I tell you? That's all you can expect of her!" or "Didn't I tell you he would act like that?" Or are we happier to confess, "I expected him to act as mean as always. But there's a kindness in him I hadn't seen until now!"?

Having good vision means having a broad awareness and a deep appreciation of what is going on around us. The difference between a pessimist and an optimist is not in what life offers them, but what they choose to see.

The difference between the irreligious and the religious is not that some have no revelations of God and others do. The revelations are here for everyone. The difference is in the beholders.

What do you see?

9

What One Person Sees Another Misses

My hat is off these days to the Great Lakes commercial fishermen. No longer do they hopefully follow an invisible path across the great waters to a favorite spot on the inland seas with the exciting expectation of loading the hold of their vessels with live, wriggling, shimmering gold. No longer do they come to port at night with fish boxes overflowing with that fork-tailed giant of the trout clan, the lake trout, and with the delectable whitefish. The villainous, blood-sucking sea lamprey and unsound conservation practices have taken an enormous toll of the Great Lakes fishing industry. (Between 1935 and 1949 in Lake Michigan alone the take of lake trout fell from a whopping 5,000,000 pounds to only 343,000 pounds. In Lake Huron the drop during the same years was from 1,743,000 pounds to a mere 1,000 pounds.) But even in these bleak and bone-bare days for commercial fishing the men still go out at dawn and return at dark, partly to protect the money and time invested in their boats and nets, but mostly because for them this is a way of life. Other work might be more lucrative. Some other jobs demand fewer hours and less risk to life and fortune. But regardless of what employment they could have if they wished, this is the way of life that has them. They belong to the fishing industry.

Men who tenaciously pursue a task that is materially unproductive and involves much risk and disappointment, a kind of occupation that most of us would shun, have an air of the heroic about them. They are doing daily what most of us would find nearly impossible. And, moreover, they illustrate a principle that we find operating throughout our experience with other people: What one person sees in life another person misses. One man's work is another man's play. Nearly everything that means a slavish, grinding drudgery to some people

is done by others with pleasure and enjoyment. The distinction between work and play is not always clear-cut and depends upon who is doing the looking. Golf is a game, a way of playing. For some commercial fishermen, however, a day on the golf links would be work of a most distasteful sort. There is too much walking in it. There are too many frustrating shots; there is too much humiliation. The golfer is too much at the mercy of an impish and contrary-minded ball and the vagaries of mischievous winds and the luck-spoiling lumps on the land. And to the golfer the fisherman's pleasure in his chores is beyond comprehension. What one person sees the other misses.

One's point of view is of tremendous importance. When a man murders a tiger, he calls it sport. But when a tiger murders a man it is called brute ferocity. Your verdict depends upon whether you have the man's or the tiger's viewpoint.

Usually pessimism and optimism are opposite ways of looking at the same thing. Two people holding these contrasting points of view see a rosebush in bloom. The grumpy one grumbles, "Isn't it a shame that God placed thorns among roses?" And the other responds, "On the contrary, isn't it wonderful that He placed roses among thorns?"

In a significant sense the supposed conflict between science and religion is a false issue. Science and religion are not *opposing* views of the meaning of our existence. They are both *fragmentary* views. What the scientist sees the religious person often overlooks. What the religious person sees the scientist frequently disregards. Science asks the quantitative questions, "How many?", "How swift?", "How heavy?" Religion asks the qualitative questions, "How lovely?", "How good?", "How worthy of my devotion and dedication?"

The scientific approach is never enough. A pre-medical student in college dated a sweet young coed for several months, and she seemed to encourage his attentions. But one night she discovered that while he was whispering endearments into her ear he kept his finger tips on her pulse, testing and then writing down her emotional reactions. That was too much science for her, and the relationship was broken.

X-ray is an excellent diagnostic instrument, but whoever carried an X-ray photograph of his girl friend or his wife in his wallet, to look at occasionally for inspiration's sake? X-ray is good science, but it is only a partial view of a person, and a mighty poor likeness at that!

On the other hand, prayer was never intended to be a substitute for X-ray, or for delicate scales, or for accurate calipers, or test tubes, or for knowledge of chemistry, physics or mechanical engineering. Religion has its limits, too. Neither science nor religion asks or answers all the questions daily life hurls at us. What one sees the other misses.

Science is a remarkable and indispensable provider for our material necessities. Through scientific agriculture the world's food production has been increased to take care of an expanding population. Scientific engineering is binding the world together with instruments of communication and transportation. Scientific medicine is prolonging life so that the average person now has a greater life expectancy than at any other time in history. But our religious faith will determine to what end we eat to stay alive, the purpose for which we live, and whether or not we have the spiritual resources to get along with each other in the new world community. What science misses religion sees.

Our understanding of the purpose and functions of denominations may rest upon our recognition that what one sees the other misses. One church sees the need for some ritual, while another overlooks it entirely. Another denomination feels the urgency of emotional response while a neighboring church frowns upon it and believes in long periods of silence before God during worship. One denomination may make much of reasoning and of intellectual validity, while another scowls at education as being of the devil and instead stresses tremendous sacrifice of one's material goods and of one's time to the Cause. And no one church is telling the whole truth about God, because the meaning of God is too big to be caught in any single creed, form, ritual or religious institution.

We are like little children playing on an ocean beach with a sand bucket. We dip our pail into the pounding surf, lift it high for all to see, and boast, "Look, everybody! I've got the ocean in my bucket!" The ocean? Not quite. A great deal of ocean has escaped our little pails.

Humility is the attitude that befits us all in a world of wonders too big for us — humility, and tolerance, too. Humility, because no one of us can see and understand everything. Always some truth lies before us, far and deep, beyond the poor capacity of our bucket-like minds. Tolerance is appropriate because someone else, with another bucket, may have caught a pailful of understanding that eluded us.

What one sees another misses.

10

Thoughts for a Rainy Day

It was a rainy Sunday afternoon in late summer. Shining silver lines of moisture slanted down from heavy skies as we drove toward our woodland retreat. Glistening bright splashes splattered upon the windshield of our car and upon the pavement and dimpled roadside puddles. The leaves of all the trees we passed looked gay and party-ready, washed by the rain and scrubbed by the brush of a stiff wind.

Some people would call it a "nasty day," for it was a picnic-spoiler, thoroughly drenching all bright plans for an outing. But as we drove up to the gate opening upon our mud-puddle-strewn trail that wanders between rain-heavy birches and apple trees to Hideaway House, we saw at the trail's edge two creatures that would not permit a downpour to upset their picnic plans. A pair of fawns stood under the dripping apple trees, browsing. They watched us nervously but without fleeing, while we stared back at them. They eyed me, between nibbles, as I stole from the car and took down the first gate-rail. I reached for the second rail and removed it. Still they stayed, alert but not panicky. Then, while laying the second pole in the grass, I accidentally knocked it against the first with a loud thud. That was enough. The fawns would tolerate our curiosity but not our noisy impertinence. They bounded away gracefully to engage in a rainy day pastime in some wooded retreat.

One reason why some of my choicest friends are animals is that they never grumble about the weather. They accept it. They adjust to it, and sometimes seem to revel in enjoyment of weather that humans call by unprintable names. There is no place on earth so cold that some creature doesn't live there, and without looking the least bit grouchy about it. The rainiest areas of the world in the tropics are inhabited by some of the gayest monkeys and liveliest birds. It is rumored that in the arid regions of the American West people have gone so long without rain that moisture is foreign to them, and that one time when a drop of water fell on a man, his buddies had to throw six buckets of sand in his face to bring him to! That's really dry! But animals are found in our Western deserts, accepting the conditions there, adjusting to them, and thriving.

What ingenious methods we use to escape the acceptance of unpleasant facts! When we blunder, we build fantastic alibis far worse than the mistakes themselves. Imperfect people marry other imperfect people, but won't accept a spouse's imperfections. Frustrated because they cannot entirely remake their partners from human beings into angels, they discard them and take up with somebody new, only to be disappointed again. They forget some things: that successful marriage is not merely a matter of *getting* the right kind of mate but also *being* the right kind; that marriage is not for angels, but human beings; and that to be human is to be imperfect. Much marital discord could be avoided if we would accept such facts.

Deeply bereaved people have been known to keep the body of a loved one in the house for weeks, not notifying authorities, and treating the body as a living person. They could not accept the fact of death. Such a flight from reality never assuages sorrow. It prolongs it. Sometimes the escape from fact leads straight to insanity.

Many a mother, aspiring to a musical career and never able to achieve it, has made herself and her child miserable by trying to compel him to take her place. She imagines he has the musical capacity that in her was never developed because of her early marriage and the rapid coming of a large family. He is goaded into spending long hours over the piano keys. He is denied boyhood pleasures because of his mother's excessive demands upon his time for practicing. When he forgets a phrase of music at a recital of pupils, or stumbles badly in his performance before house guests, he is made to feel guilty. He has let his mother down, bringing her grief and shame. She never guesses that his talent doesn't lie in music, but possibly in woodworking, or scientific experimentation, or in mathematics. Her wish that he would fulfill her own frustrated ambitions for the concert stage has blinded her to what he is. The result is a miserable mother and son, and the stunting of a real talent in some area other than music. A person who cannot accept unalterable fact is a menace to self and to others.

Some people suffer irreparable damage because they cannot accept the superiority of another person. They rush into financial ruin trying to "keep up with the Joneses," when they don't have the Joneses' money resources. With much less income than Old Man Jones, they spend almost as much as he for cars, clothes, and entertainment. At long last insolvency follows unless they come to their senses and simply admit that the Joneses are financially superior to them and therefore can afford to live "higher off the hog."

Many a highway wreck is caused by a driver who cannot tolerate having another car ahead of him on the road. If the driver ahead is going fifty miles an hour, he must be passed. But if he's travelling eighty, he still must be passed. Some drivers cannot accept the fact that there will *always* be someone ahead on the road.

So with life. Few ever reach the top rung in the ladder of excellency. If you run, there will be someone in the world who can outrun you. If you box, there is someone who can beat you, if not now, very soon. Read the sports pages and see the champions fall! If you shine intellectually, there is someone, somewhere, who can out-think you. If you teach or preach, if you swim or shoot, if you joke or pray, if you win friends or sell products, there is someone in your world, probably not far from you, who is your superior.

What of it? Supposing you cannot be the world's champion in your field. If you can't beat the champ, there is one important opponent over whom you can triumph. You cannot always be better than someone else. But you can be better than the person you were yesterday.

Whenever we refuse to face facts, whether they are the weather, our own limitations, or the imperfections of others, a great emergency or tragedy, or the superior accomplishments of others — whenever we stubbornly reject reality we defeat ourselves.

God has given us a strangely mixed world with hard, sharp facts amidst our joys like thorns amidst roses and with depressing drizzles falling between days of glorious radiance. But it is His world and it is His way. We find our peace and poise in accepting thorns while rejoicing in flowers, and in accepting rain while delighting in sunshine.

11

Living Above Necessity

There are some things a person must do to stay alive. Eating and drinking, exercising and resting, inhaling and exhaling — all are sheerest necessities. But how barren life would be if we engaged only in necessary activities and knew nothing of the excitement of an occasional luxury or a rare surprise. How flat and tasteless life would be if we could not, for an occasional few moments, live above mere necessity.

One warm summer afternoon, feeling an urge for strenuous exercise, I decided to clear a much-needed trail along our brook. The brush was thick. Low-hanging limbs tore at our guests, playfully snatching off their hats and mischievously poking woody fingers in their eyes and ears. Taking my hatchet, I plunged into the tough network of brush and branches, chopping away industriously for half an hour or so. As I paused for a moment's rest and a deep inhalation of the woodsy air, I heard an unfamiliar hammering in a brookside glade not far away. The sound was surely that of a woodpecker searching beneath old bark for a mid-afternoon snack of grubs or beetles. But the mighty pounding was too great to be made by a red-headed woodpecker or a downy woodpecker or any of the woodpecker tribe familiar to me. As I crept from a woodland thicket toward the opening from which the drumming came, a flashing red crest caught my eyes, and I saw a pileated woodpecker, rare in this country, digging deep, rectangular-shaped holes in a dying tree. So preoccupied was he with his work that I stood unnoticed, watching him while he riddled the tree's south side with gaping cavities. Then, satisfied with his repast, he flew to some haunt unknown to me, never to return so far as I know. That day offered me a bonus, an unexpected treat. I had left the cabin to get needed exercise and to perform a necessary task. But before the hour was over I was enjoying

-KOHN-a luxury, feasting my eyes and gratifying my thoughts with one of life's "extras." For a few moments I had lived above necessity.

A person could hardly be familiar with nature and miss the evidences that this world is full of luxuries. Everywhere in creation the Planner has gone far beyond sheer necessity, filling life with extras. Could not the Creator have made some sort of law-abiding universe without extra adornments of breathtaking beauty? It would seem so. Yet, while the barest necessities are here, added to them are rich flourishes of loveliness as if the Designer had said, as He fashioned the universe and provided all the essentials, "Now, these are for creation's sake." Then, adding beauty, He said, "And this is for love's sake."

For example, a world like ours needs sunrises and sunsets — sunrises so that a cold, dark earth can be bathed in warmth and energy and light, and sunsets so that the earth might have some rest from the continuous beating of the sun's rays upon its surface and so that all life might not be burnt to a sizzling crisp. Yes, sunrises and sunsets are necessary to the maintenance of this kind of an earth. But why the soft gray-greens of early dawns and the multicolored hues of evening skies, as if the Heavenly Artist had plunged His brush deep into a colorful imagination and with joyfully careless strokes had splashed the earth's horizons? Why?

Have you ever seen an enlarged photograph of a snowflake? Have you examined a freshly-fallen snowflake under a microscope? If you have, you are no stranger to the way God fills the natural world with extras. Each snowflake differs from every other snowflake. Yet each is a bit of crystalline perfection, demonstrating the skill of an infinitely patient and painstaking Craftsman who has played for millennia upon the theme of six-sidedness without making two flakes alike. Would snow not be fully as useful if it were not so carefully designed, perhaps made in irregular forms like torn-off bits of cottonbatten? It would still cover the cold regions of the earth with a protective blanket. It could still melt in springtime, giving the thirsty earth a long, much-needed drink. But snowflakes are evidences of what our spiritual forebears called "God's grace," which they interpreted to be the "unmerited favor" that comes to us. We get more than we need and more than we deserve. We are the recipients of "extras."

Much Christian religion stresses too heavily the justice of God, as if the symbol of the faith were not a cross of love, but delicately balanced scales where God weighed rewards according to our merit. Justice is a part of God's nature, but the New Testament and human experience alike witness to the predominant trait of the Almighty — "God is love." We are not treated justly by God. If anyone doubts that, then let him dare to pray earnestly, "Give me what I deserve." Extra blessings far exceeding our merits pour down on all of us. Whether we love God or heed Him, His sun warms us and His returning seasons of seedtime, growth, and harvest feed us. Countless good things daily come our way that we have not asked for nor earned.

An awareness of the extras life affords us ought to do us some positive good. For one thing, it should make us more grateful than we are. When trouble comes our way, what is our most familiar complaint? It goes something like this: "What have I done to deserve all this?" Supposing we continue to ask that question, but under different circumstances. When life is good to us, then let us ask, "What have I done to deserve all this?" On Memorial Day, the Fourth of July, or any other patriotic occasion, when we commemorate the valiant deaths of those we have never seen but who died that we might have a great, free nation, let's ask that question, "What have I done to deserve all this?"

On Mother's Day and Father's Day, on wedding anniversaries and birthdays, occasions when we are reminded of what others mean to us, or when we are amidst friends who love and trust us and seek our company, let us ask, "What have I done to deserve this?" A survey of the unearned extras that we receive will make us more grateful.

Moreover, this understanding of God's grace, this consciousness of unmerited mercies coming our way, can help us set up a standard for our treatment of other people. Because I have been treated by God far better than I deserve, I shall always deal with others gracefully, treating them better than justice demands. A coolly calculated sense of justice is not enough if we are to serve the world. Merely seeking out those who are good and being good to them will never do. The worst, too, need a taste of the best. Be God-like. Give to people much more than they demand or deserve.

Few secrets of living make life so flavorful as living above necessity.

12

When It Happens to You

The golden flaky flesh of brown trout decorated our dinner plates last night and tickled our palates. The trout would have been tasty in any case, whether donated by a thoughtful neighbor, purchased from a store, or eaten at a restaurant. But they were better than the best that could have come from any other source, because they were our own trout, caught on our own lines, in our own brook. We had a personal feeling toward those delectable fish. They happened to us. And a trout with whom you have matched wits, whose dashing energy you have felt surging at the end of your line, a trout whose tail-beating you have heard against the inside of your creel, a trout you have cleaned and iced and fried is always the tastiest of trout. It's because such a fish is more than a fish. It is *your* fish.

Each summer the newspapers and magazines feature photographs of our President fishing. This year President Eisenhower was shown kneedeep in a swift Western mountain stream, and again in apron bending over an outdoor fireplace, serving up his freshly fried trout to fellow campers. He loves to eat fish. But the President, like the rest of us, loves most the taste of a trout that has fought at the end of his own line.

There are at least two ways of knowing anything. We can know the *facts* about a thing, such as that a brown trout is a fish, that it is yellow-brown in color with blue-bordered red spots dotting its sides, that it spawns in the fall, and that its tribe was introduced to America from Europe in the last century. But besides the facts, we can know the *influence* of a thing, like the way a brown trout lures a man to a stream's bank, and playfully tests his fishing prowess, and plunges powerfully as it seeks to escape, making the line sing and the spine tingle, and pounds a lively tattoo on the inside of the creel, and the way a forkful of trout melts in the mouth and snuggles down comfortably in the stomach. There is a profound difference between knowing the facts about trout and feeling a trout's influence.

A chemist, lost and wandering in the desert, crazed with thirst, can mumble between parched and cracked lips the chemical formula for water. The facts he knows full well. But the facts won't save him. He yearns to feel the influence of water, the refreshment sweeping over him as water pours down his throat, washing the heat from his tissues and the madness from his brain. Only the influence of water will help him.

How unaffected we often are by learning facts! Our newspapers are filled with stories about someone else's disasters and joys. We read of auto accidents and hunting tragedies and of sicknesses. We learn of engagements and marriages and births. We are but slightly affected by the news. Then someone near us becomes involved: your brother lies near death with his chest crushed by a broken steering wheel, or a neighbor lad is accidentally shot while hunting, or your son's temperature soars to one hundred and four degrees and hovers there for days. Your daughter becomes engaged, or your own name appears in the wedding announcements, or your own child is born. Then we know a thing as more than a fact. It is an influence, a power.

We can take pain in our stride. Sure thing! If it's someone else's pain. We can give glib advice on how to handle grief — someone else's grief. We know how to face the facts — if the facts are happening to others. But until a fact becomes *my* fact I never feel its full weight nor sense its importance.

Knowing the truth about people is a paltry thing when compared with knowing the people themselves, feeling the consequences of their friendship upon our lives. And isn't this a primary difference between religious philosophy and religious experience? Religious philosophy is thinking *about* God. Religious experience is *knowing* God, feeling the upward tug of His influence.

Few differences in this world are so impressive as the differences between knowing a thing has happened and knowing it has happened to you.

13

As Free As a Bird?

When I was a small lad and greatly impressed by, and inclined to ponder over, the words and phrases used by my elders, an expression frequently spoken by people around me lodged deep in my mind. When someone was given a few days' vacation from work, or when a mortgage was paid, or when a burdensome duty had been performed, this exclamation was made: "I feel as free as a bird!"

This spring when tree swallows took up summer quarters in our martin house, I had occasion to review the meaning of the phrase, "as free as a bird." From the perches built around their new abode they would launch themselves into swooping, soaring, gliding flight out over Lake Charlevoix. Sunlight glistened upon them, and the soft sheen of their backs glowed in blue and metallic green as they hunted for flying insects, their staple food. Then, one by one, they would return to the bird house again, descending from a great height or arising from near the water's surface where they had skimmed off hatching aquatic flies. These gay and uninhibited birds go and come as they please, eat when they're hungry, punch no time clock, answer to no employers, pay no taxes. To first appearance our swallow neighbors seem to have what mankind everywhere is yearning for — absolute freedom.

But the freedom of a swallow is a relative thing and something of an illusion. A tree swallow is free to plow the air with keen-edged wings and turn up insects for its meals. But it is not free to eat fish like a gull if insects should prove scarce, nor free to eat birds' eggs as does a crow. Its bill is not adapted to the task of catching fish or breaking egg shells.

A tree swallow is free to usurp a martin house if it can beat the martins to the door and hold it against all comers. But if martin houses and tree holes and hollow fence posts and other

ready-made houses should prove unavailable, a tree swallow is not free to build nests on the tips of swaying branches as is the Baltimore oriole, nor upon an open gravel bank as will a killdeer. The instincts of a tree swallow have not prepared it for *all* emergencies.

Free as a tree swallow may be to come northward with the spring when insects become plentiful, and fly southward in the fall when insects die or hibernate, our winged neighbor is not free to leave its troubles behind. The appearance of perfect freedom is an illusion, and wherever a tree swallow goes it is a captive of its restricted diet, in bondage to its inherited instincts, limited by its environment, and confined to a few years of time under the arching sky.

A casual glance at nature impresses the onlooker with the freedom of all wild things, but a more thorough familiarity with the natural order convinces the student that all creation is under a discipline. Planets are not free to roam wildly through the universe. They are confined to their appointed courses. Birds are free to act like birds, and birds of a certain species are at liberty to behave like their breed. But tree swallows cannot act like elephants, nor even imitate a ruffed grouse, which is a not-too-distant relative. A trillium plant may be free to spread its offspring through a shady, moist forest glade, but it is not free to look like a yellow lady-slipper nor to smell like an apple blossom. If we mean by freedom the capacity for a thing to be or do anything, just anything at all, there is no such thing as freedom.

Moreover, even if it could be had, absolute freedom for everyone and everything would be most undesirable. Free flowage of water is water in flood stage without confining banks. Free-sweeping fire is a fire out of control, murderous and devastating. Freedom for everyone means freedom for criminals to make their attacks and plunder, and for dictators to work their diabolic will.

The history of advancing civilization is largely the story of free forces submitting to discipline. Modern farming is the result of man's gathering wild leaf, root, bulb, and grain crops, bringing them into captivity, taming them, and keeping them in limited fields. Wild animals also have been domesticated, some being used as pets and others for milk, meat, clothing or transportation.

The conquest and discipline of fire was one of the first steps in the expansion of civilization. It enabled prehistoric man to move from semi-tropical climates to chillier regions and still keep warm. Fire provided a means for cooking food, making it tastier and easier to chew and to digest. Fire was probably the first wild power in nature to be brought under man's control. Once found only in forest fires begun by lightning, or at the edge of volcanoes, once only a force for destruction, when tamed it became an efficient and helpful servant.

Much of the industrial revolution of the eighteenth and nineteenth centuries, that resulted in a higher standard of living for millions and the building of big businesses and big cities, resulted from the invention of the steam engine. And the steam engine is only a mechanism for using power by capturing it and disciplining it. A cubic foot of boiling water expands into about 1,700 cubic feet of steam, and when the expanding molecules of steam are confined within the walls of a closed container, they exert a tremendous force which is converted into mechanical power. While steam rising free into the atmosphere is weak, steam that is disciplined is strong.

Gasoline lying spilled upon the pavement is as free as gasoline could be, but it is without power. When poured into the tank of an automobile, gasoline is still powerless. This fuel becomes powerful when it moves from the roominess of the tank to the narrow confines of the motor, where it is made captive of the piston cylinders and ignited and exploded under pressure. Free-flowing gasoline is weak. Gasoline brought under the mastery of the motor is strong to turn crankshafts, gears and wheels.

A piano key can be broken off the keyboard where it is held captive and freed from its bondage. Then the key can be rolled about on the floor, tossed into the air, or lie free on a table. It has its freedom. But it is no longer free to accomplish the purpose for which it was made. It is not free to make music in harmony with its companions of the keyboard. Let it be returned to its proper place and be bound once more to the piano. Then alone is it really free to fulfill its purpose for being — free to sing.

Here lies an essential difference between formal and personal religion. In formal religion one masters the subject matter, learns the creeds, becomes properly catechized, studies when and how to genuflect and go through all the proper motions and how to say the proper words. By so doing a person may become a master of religion. But when religion becomes profoundly personal, one is no longer so much a master of religion, but mastered *by* it. Religion is not then a mere matter of learning and understanding. Dedication has been added.

Wilfred Grenfell, the famed heroic missionary to Labrador, when still a young doctor, was congratulated by a friend who exclaimed, "Dr. Grenfell, I hear you've got religion."

"No," answered Grenfell, "religion's got me!"

We are at our best when we are dedicated to the Highest and under His control.

14

The Big Assurances

On these Lake Charlevoix shores, where waves whisper secrets to killdeers at play, and soft summer breezes collect wild scents and bring them as friendly offerings to our door, and the emerald waters dance beneath the blue immensity of the sky, it is easy to believe in the greatness of God. There is little here that is human, or that the human mind could invent or the human hand fashion. The natural world is obviously a created world, and the Creator plainly excels man's skills and his wisdom and might.

One of the chief reasons why we are an anxious and fear-ridden generation is that we live in a man-made civilization. Upon every hand we are surrounded with what man has created—sky-scraping buildings, rushing automobiles, spreading ribbons of concrete, machine-made and machine-run homes, machine-made clothes, machine-processed foods, machine-made necessities and machine-made luxuries, and man-made machines. Even the country-dweller, once so "close to nature," now works with power tools, lives in a gadget-controlled house, and is surrounded with factory-made conveniences.

Depending so entirely upon human ingenuity for his necessities and comforts, is it any wonder that the twentieth-century person is anxious and filled with foreboding? His world seems to be man's doing. He dwells in a man-centered civilization. And yet he is aware that the earth's chaos, the seering slaughter of war has been man's doing, too. Now, with earth-shattering weapons in his trembling, fumbling hands, blundering man seems to control the future. Such a future seems bleak, hellish. As someone has rephrased a familiar proverb, "The road to hell is paved with good inventions." Our technical advances have outdistanced our souls, and we are not sure we can catch up in time.

In spite of a high record in church attendance these days, we are also piling up unmatched statistics in numbers of sleeping pills and tranquilizer tablets and headache potions consumed. There is a high rate of psychosomatic diseases, of suicides and admissions to mental hospitals. Why is our religion doing us so little good? What has happened to our capacity for inner peace? What has become of the big assurances that once made for a spirit of trust, even among the hard-pressed and troubled?

Our distress is due, at least in part, to having a cut-flower religion, where we have any religion at all. We try to maintain our faith, our belief, our trust, apart from the experiences in which they were once rooted. When we do this, our beliefs and faiths and trusts — without rootage — wither and die.

Many of the big assurances that once made for trustful living were deeply rooted in man's observation of nature. From his experiences of creation the sensitive soul developed a faith in the Creator. Nature had a sacramental meaning to him, presenting outward and visible signs of an inner and spiritual presence.

It was natural for the farmer to develop a profound faith in God's dependability. He saw that the seasons moved in a reliable succession. Autumn always followed summer. He could count on winter succeeding autumn. And no matter how long and bleak winter might be, some bright day the last snow would melt. Brooks would swell and overflow. Silver-gray pussy-willows would emerge from their long sleep. Drowsy bees would drift along on warm breezes. Winter would be at an end. Spring would come. He could depend, too, on carrot seed growing into carrots and not into cabbages, and horses having foals and not calves, and chickens hatching chicks from their eggs and not ducklings. While there were unaccountables enough in farming—the vagaries of weather, capricious winds, mysterious diseases afflicting crops and flocks and herds—it was the basic dependabilities in nature that made farming possible. To his belief in these the husbandman clung, and from these he inferred trustworthiness as an attribute of his God. That God could be counted upon was one of the big assurances by which farmers lived and worked.

The planter and herdsman knew the meaning of patient and

trustful waiting upon God's power and goodness. When he had planted his seed there was nothing more a farmer could do but to wait for a Power beyond himself, whose servants were sun and rain and fertility of soil, to perform for him what he could not achieve for himself. Only when these forces beyond the farmer's control had discharged their duties would seeds sprout and grain grow. When a herdsman's cattle and sheep were bred there was no way of hurrying the advent of their young. Calves and lambs would come in due time, but not before time. One must wait for a slow development that man could not hasten nor direct. It was one of man's big assurances that he could afford to wait for God.

One is tempted to say that we need in our time as much faith as our forefathers had in their day. But that is not so. One thing we do not need in our generation is more faith. We have *too much* faith already — in the wrong things. Much of personal foolishness and international folly is due to our super-abundance of trust, invested in all sorts of nostrums ranging from rabbit's feet and astrology to money, dictatorships, and ill-conceived schemes for putting an end to war. We don't need more faith. The great want is for the investment of such faith as we already possess in the principles that make for inner peace and social concord. And for these basic truths we can do no better than to search where Jesus and the great teachers of all time found them — in nature.

One of the big assurances expressed by nature is that God cares for all His creatures. As Alfred North Whitehead, the Harvard philosopher, put it: "The image under which the nature of God can best be conceived is that of a tender care that nothing be lost." And long before Whitehead, another Teacher said, "Are not five sparrows sold for two farthings, and not one of them is forgotten before God? But even the very hairs of your head are all numbered. Fear not therefore: ye are of more value than many sparrows." A walk through a woods will convince an observer that this pronouncement of philosophy and religion has wide application. Nothing in a forest is ever lost. Many things are transformed — but nothing is lost. Leaves fall. Ferns wither and drop to the forest floor. Birds and animals die, and all are gathered to the earth, transformed into humus, and become the life-stuff of future generations of vegetable and animal life. Water evaporates from a woodland pond and disappears into the atmosphere, but it is not lost. Transformed into water vapor, it has ascended, and will sometime descend as rain to refresh a thirsty earth. Wherever we go in God's world, we see all things being transformed, but nothing lost, not even a sparrow, a hair, a fallen leaf, or a molecule of water vapor. That is one of nature's assurances of what God is like. We can trust a God like that.

Again, nature demonstrates that the Creator has so fashioned this universe that the best can emerge from the worst. Where forest fires once raged, jack pines and birches now thrive. The stubborn cones of jack pine often remain tightly closed, withholding their seeds from the soil until fire forces them open. As a consequence, fire has given some jack pines their only chance to get started on the earth. White birch crave open places where they can get light and air for growth. Fire burns such openings into the forest and gives white birches their opportunity . During World War II ninety-five types of flowers and shrubs unknown for decades were found in London, in holes where nitrates from bursting and burning bombs had enriched the soil. Seeds of grain are freed to multiply in the soil when the wind has whipped them or the threshing machine has threshed them. The pearl in an oyster is formed when an irritant, such as a grain of sand, causes the oyster to secrete a soothing substance around the aggravation. The secretion becomes a jewel. A moth's wings are strengthened for flight when the creature struggles to get free of its imprisoning cocoon; no struggle, no strength. Nature is rife with trouble that ends in blessing. One of the big assurances that this created world offers us is that trouble can be made to serve high purposes.

Once more, nature reminds us that this earth is a growing and changing place. Look around you and see. Seeds sprout and grow into plants. Saplings become trees. Fingerlings become game fish. Cubs becomes foxes or bears. Puppies grow into dogs, kittens into cats, children into adults. Nothing is meant to stay the way it is. For you who do not want to stay the way you are, nature is reassuring you that you need not remain as you are. Indeed you *cannot* remain as you are. All things must change, including you. What is important is the direction in which you change.

Moreover, nature witnesses to the great assurance that we are surrounded with inexhaustible resources. We may fail to use them intelligently, but they never fail us. There is more air in the atmosphere than we can breathe. There is more interesting, exciting, and mysterious activity going on in the earth beneath our feet, in the grasses and flowers, shrubs and trees, and in the heavens above us, than we can ever be attentive to or understand. The earth has springs too deep and abundant ever to dry up. You are in the midst of an abundance beyond your need.

We live in a universe that is intelligible and sacramental. The things we see testify to verities that are unseen but nevertheless real, just as a visible handclasp may denote an invisible feeling of friendship. Creation witnesses to what the Creator is like — dependable, caring, so imaginative and resourceful as to make the best of the worst, providing us with capacity for change and growth and with resources of power beyond our need. If that is what God is like, we can live trustfully.

15

Some Essentials

It is always easy to believe that one's specialty is life's highest good.

The French critic, Vinet, once said, "Most friends of the truth love it as Frederick the Great loved music. It used to be said of him that, strictly speaking, he was not fond of music but of the flute, and not indeed fond of the flute, but of *his* flute." In numberless ways our minds work like that of Frederick the Great. We do not so much believe in political parties as in "my" political party, not so much in religion as in "my" religion, not so much in churches as in "my" church, nor so much in truth-seeking as in defending "my" little segment of the truth as the whole truth.

Whatever we look upon steadily can grow to an all-encompassing importance in our minds. For example, this evening I have been reflecting upon the importance of rocks until, if I would allow it, rocks would assume cosmic importance and seem to be the essence from which all life stems. This contemplation began as I looked out my study window toward the bay and saw that the lowering water level of Lake Charlevoix had uncovered still more rocks along the shore. Rocks have always been there, as long as human memory can recall, but just now the shore seems unusually lumpy with water-rounded stones.

A few yards farther down the beach, rocks have been ground to fine sand by the weathering of the ages, and prankish breezes and playful waves have piled the sands in long rippling rows. Still farther in the distance lies our town built upon a thin coverlet of soil laid over rock. And beyond Charlevoix rest the rolling hills made of rocks with a sprinkling of soil upon them and mighty Lake Michigan, stored in an immense stone cup.

A geologist can make a good case for rocks being the backbone of our earth and all life here. He asks, "What is our earth but one gigantic ball of rock, molten at the center and hard on the outside?" The soils from which our food-plants grow are crumbled or weathered rock mixed with a bit of decayed animal matter. Plants get their food from this source, food that is held in suspension by moisture in the soil. Animals, including human beings, eat the plants, assimilating the earth's minerals which were once absorbed by the plants. Those animals, like cougars, that eat almost nothing but meat receive their necessary quota of minerals from the earth, for they devour animals, like deer, sheep, and rabbits, which are plant eaters. When we see that all human life and animal life depends, directly or indirectly, on plant life, and plant life depends upon the soil, and soil depends upon the rocks from which it is worn or dissolved, we can understand why the geologist looks upon rocks as one of life's basic essentials. And when we realize that man's first tools were made of stone, and that our present-day civilization is symbolized by skyscrapers and paved roads made of concrete (man-made rock), and that stone is used in hundreds of everyday conveniences from grindstones and knife-sharpeners to tooth powder, we are inclined to agree with the geologist.

The enthusiastic chemist, too, is one who is apt to love *his* truth, to see the world as essentially one vast chemical laboratory. He will inform you that chemistry, the study of the composition of matter, gets to the heart of things. Matter, he will say, is anything which has mass or weight and which occupies space. That includes nearly everything from the distant sun to the air you breathe and the nature of your own body. With the aid of astronomical instruments chemists have analyzed the composition of the sun. With weights and measurements they have reduced the chemical composition of the human body to the following ingredients:

Enough water (hydrogen and oxygen) to fill a ten-gallon can
Enough fat to manufacture seven bars of soap
Carbon enough to make nine thousand lead pencils
Iron for two nails
Enough phosphorus for two thousand, two hundred matches
Enough lime to whitewash a good-sized chicken coop
Mere sprinklings of several other chemicals such as magnesium, potassium, sodium and sulphur

And what of the rocks which lie on the lake's edge and form the hills and the earth's core? The chemist says they are his business too, since they have mass and weight and occupy space.

To the chemist all life is apt to be seen as essentially chemical composition and chemical reaction. To the geologist life stems from the rocks. Yet, to the person unversed in geology and chemistry neither of these aspects of our world seems to be so fundamental.

Being neither a geologist nor a chemist, I am not apt to see the world's basic essentials as rocks or chemical components. But like everyone else I am sure to regard *something* as fundamental, and to me the essence of life is spiritual. Before there was a material universe here, there was a Spirit to plan and to fashion it. Spirit is first and last, undergirding and pervading all things, the ultimate Reality upon which all else depends. My first principles, therefore, are spiritual in nature.

Reflecting for a few moments upon what I consider to be life's basic essentials, I find the following are among the most fundamental (although I do not list them in order of their importance):

To live in such a way as to have nothing I wish to hide from God or man

To be tough with myself and tender with others

To face unpleasant facts unflinchingly

To love mankind all-inclusively

To have the eyes and mind of Christ—seeing the glory in commonplace things and "ordinary" people

To be tolerant of others' religious and philosophical positions, knowing we may share the same experiences without having the same explanations of them

To live above minimums, doing more for the world than is demanded of me

To seek always the happiness and welfare of the greatest number

To reflect well on what I am going to say rather than regret what I have said.

To work for high purposes rather than mainly for money

To sacrifice wholeheartedly for those things in which I believe

To work hard in the knowledge that achievement comes from perspiration as well as inspiration

To attend to the little things, knowing the big things depend upon the little ones

To live gratefully without grumbling complaint

To use the material things of my life for great purposes, being ever aware that things temporal are ennobled by their participation in things eternal

To accept criticism graciously, knowing that if it is false it can do me no lasting harm, and if true it will forewarn me against future failure

To live at an unhurried pace, remembering that haste and spiritual culture are sworn enemies

To make the most of the time God grants me here and to make the most of the place where I spend that time

To keep my purposes simple and my mind uncluttered and well organized

To think of, believe in, and live by mighty themes

To have the courage to conform to nothing save the pattern I believe the Almighty has in mind for me

To put manhood first, preferring to be a good man before being a good minister, or good writer, or artist, or even a good husband and father, remembering that even God had to make man before He could make him into the head of a family or a craftsman or a professional or a Christian

To be humble, recognizing that what I do not know transcends what I know, that I am not a source of good but a channel through which it can flow, and that I am always dispensable, that the world can very well get along without me (and some day will!)

To seek constantly for more mind-stretching, soul-enlarging information about the universe and its Creator

To see the world and its people in terms of what they are capable of becoming and to be fully committed to help fulfill those possibilities

To live out of an abundance of spiritual resources, to be an artesian sort of person with wells of strength beyond my own needs so that others can refresh themselves from my supply

To pay rent for the space allowed me while on earth by making the world a bit better because I have been here

To spend my life doing something that will outlast it

To be so linked with the Eternal, who is bigger than myself and more important than my own fortunes, so that what happens to me will seem of minor moment, and what happens to His Cause of major importance

When I have done my best, to leave the outcome in God's capable hands.

- KOHN -

16

Use It or Lose It

There's a world of difference between a wild animal and a tame one. As a child I often saw raccoons in the city zoo, sullen, lazy, dyspeptic creatures. But the raccoons that make Hidden Brook their home and raid our garbage can, turning it topsy-turvy with a great clang and clatter soon after darkness falls — these raccoons are far removed from their caged and pampered relatives. They are crafty, sharp-witted, nimble, excitable. Masters of every trick for evading hunting packs of coon dogs, they wade along creeks, walk fallen logs, and dive into lakes to lose their scent and frustrate their pursuers. They are resourceful hunters of food. Rocks, when turned over, prove hiding places for snails, mussels, and water insects. Long, black, dextrous raccoon fingers dart after frogs and fishes. White grubs are grabbed from rotting logs, pulled apart by strong raccoon claws. Mice are caught. Turtle eggs are smelled out, dug up and devoured. Corn from farmers' fields and grains and fruits are picked when fall comes. A wild raccoon is an alert, intelligent creature with his wits working wonderfully to keep him alive and fat. A tame raccoon, while an affectionate and mischievous pet, has the keen edges of his senses dulled by man's protection. Unused wits are soon lost.

When any wild animal accustomed to staying alive by constant use of its intelligence is captured and protected by man, it tends to lose some of its mental faculties. Such a change can take place in a single generation as recent experiments in Germany have demonstrated. A German zoologist caught a pair of wild foxes and confined them to a zoo, where they were sheltered, fed, and protected from hunters and their dogs. The vixen littered and some of the young foxes, when partly grown, were released to run wild again. These too produced young. The zoologist, having caught and killed some members of three generations, weighed their brains and recorded amazing results. The original wild generation had brains weighing fifty grams. The brains of the generation born and reared in the zoo weighed only thirty-five grams. Brains of the second wild generation weighed fifty grams. Concerning creatures' wits Nature has decreed, "Use them or lose them."

In nearly all species of animals and birds that man has domesticated the muzzle and the skull have grown shorter than in their wild relatives. Why does the muzzle shrink? Because man prepares the creature's food for him, reducing the work that jaws and teeth must do. With a decreased work load, these members shrink to fit their task. The skulls grow shorter because the animals and birds are protected by man from their natural enemies and are sheltered from bad weather. They need not use their fully developed senses, so those parts of the brain that have to do with seeing, hearing, and smelling become dull and underdeveloped. Senses that are used little develop little. Senses that are wholly unused are lost at last.

The biological law of atrophy with disuse has its counterpart in man's spiritual, intellectual, and moral life. Every potential we have must be employed or it degenerates. Those who constantly use their capacities for reverence, seeking out the highest and holiest in public worship, private prayer, in nature and history and in the lives of their fellowmen, find reverence growing. But those who use it slightly have little of it. We use it or lose it.

A little human understanding, compassion, and kindness utilized daily will grow. Unused, it is lost until not a vestige is apparent in one's dealings with his fellows.

An active conscience stays alive and vital. A shunned conscience soon withers from want of exercise and dies.

Long ago Alexander Pope put this principle in memorable words:

"The wasting moth ne'er spoiled my best array;
The cause was this, I wore it every day."

All the way from Hidden Brook raccoon to you, all creatures and all capacities are under Nature's law: Use it or lose it.

86

17

On Having Boundaries

There is only a slight difference between a river and a swamp. While both are watery, a river is limited, disciplined by its banks, whereas the wetness of a swamp is free to spread out in a relatively unrestricted way.

But this little difference makes for big consequences. Swamps stand in the way of human progress. They preclude the possibility of agriculture unless expensive drainage can be performed. They force deviation of roads from the most economical route — a straight-line path — for the cost of building roads over marshy ground usually proves prohibitively high. But when water is confined between banks and disciplined to flow in a specific direction and along a definite path it becomes a servant to civilization.

Rivers carrying rich soil from wide continental interiors and depositing it in deltas along the rivers' mouths make for some of the world's most fertile farm land.

For thousands of years energy derived from swiftly flowing streams has been used by man, in the Nile Valley of Africa, in India and in China, for driving man's machines and doing his work. Still, in our own time, man harnesses the Tennessee River, the Colorado, Columbia, and Niagara rivers to turn his turbines and provide him with electrical power.

For ages past, and in our own day as well, men have been using rivers as natural routes for traveling and carrying cargo. Many of the ancient explorations of the Old World and modern discoveries in the New World were made by boat on the earth's big streams. Especially were the river arteries of North America the means by which new life flowed into this continent. Early navigators did not always cast anchor upon reaching American shores, for the great streams flowing from the interior of the continent invited them onward. Many rivers were navigable

for several miles — the Hudson, the Connecticut, the Raritan, the Susquehanna, the Rappahannock, the Potomac, the York, the James, the Roanoke, the Santee being among the numerous streams wide enough and deep enough for ocean-going vessels of colonial times. Other smaller streams would accommodate the shallop and canoe.

It was at river mouths and along river banks that the first towns were established, and rivers were watery highways of communication between the first outposts of European civilization in America. Great-great-great-grandfathers of our friendly neighbor chickadees called down cheery greetings to small expeditions of the white men when they first came into the Great Lakes region and felt along these shores and nosed their dugouts and canoes up Michigan streams.

Swamps, free and undisciplined stretches of wetness, have stood in the way of man's progress. Rivers, water confined between banks and limited in freedom, have helped man on his way toward a higher civilization.

Some lives are swampy. They fret and chafe under restraint and evade self-discipline. They get nowhere.

Other people are river-like. Knowing that without discipline there can be no real achievement, they submit to control as a stream submits to its banks.

Some busy people are ineffectual because their "busyness" is spread out in every direction in general and aimed at nothing in particular. They put in long hours; they consume vast amounts of energy; they are in a constant dither and make quite a show of always doing something, but alas, nothing of lasting value. Then there are the river-like workers whose energies and emotions are confined within the limits of a single purpose worthy of their wholehearted devotions. They are going somewhere.

A profound liking for people on the one hand and a desire to serve them on the other gives life some noble restraints, keeping conversation from spreading into slander, preventing self-pride from expanding into envy over another's successes, restraining one from exploiting another's weaknesses.

The person who, like the sensualist, wants his affections to be free and undisciplined, with no limitations whatsoever, has a swampy conception of love. Love, to have value, must be selective. One cannot successfully love everything indiscriminately and equally. Some things are worthy of our highest love, as God is. Other things merit everlasting love, as our mates do. Others deserve our love interpreted as "goodwill in action," as our neighbors and enemies do. Still other things, money and material possessions, should have our attention but without any attachment or final loyalty or deep affection. Undisciplined love, like unrestrained water, is swampy. Disciplined love, confined to the highest values, is like a river, going somewhere and performing services.

Everyone owes it to himself to take an occasional inventory of his life and ask of his heart, "What am I, swamp or stream?"

18

The Glory of Organization

A brook's edge, one would think, might be a most muddled
and confused place. Thrown together there one can find a wide
disparity of natural objects — flowing water and inert land,
growing grasses and lifeless stones, high-strung deer and lethargic
trees — a miscellany of living and non-living things heaped together in a scrambled hodge-podge.

Yet, the border of a brook, far from being a disturbing
disorder of unrelated objects, is a highly organized miniature
universe, where everything works together with everything else
in a harmonious manner. Water bathes the banks with life-
giving moisture, and the stream's banks cradle the creek, giving
it form and security. Vegetation receives nutriment from the
soil and in return binds the soil in its place, hindering erosion.
The root hairs of the birches drink deeply from brook waters,
while birch foliage shades the stream from the sun's hot rays,
preventing excessive evaporation. Deer sip from the crystal
waters and feed on the dense, rich marginal browse, while they
exhale carbon dioxide breathed by green plants and used in
the manufacture of their starches. Trout make the stream their
home and pay for their room and board by helping to maintain
a balance of life in the waters, limiting the number of insects, crustaceans, and other fishes to be found there. Although
composed of a multiplicity of creatures, a stream-side environment is saved from confusion by its high degree of organization.

The splendor of almost anything can be traced to its organization. Physicists inform us that when certain atoms are grouped
together in one way they make a lump of coal, but the same
atoms arranged in a different way make a diamond. It isn't
the *number* of atoms that determines the difference between
coal and diamond, but how they are organized. Great music
is composed of separate sounds which any fool can make.

But those individual sounds make glorious music only when a musical genius organizes them into a composition. Great art is the organization of form, line and color, and great literature the masterly arrangement of words.

What makes great living possible? Examine the lives of humanity's towering benefactors and you will find they had this in common: all organized their living around a supreme value or purpose. They put that first, at the center. Then all other matters were arranged around that value according to their comparative significance. And when seen in the light of one big purpose, some things had no importance at all.

In his youth, Abraham Lincoln was a confused person, the victim and center of emotional storms that threatened to blow him apart. He didn't know what to do with himself or for others. Criticism hurt him deeply. When Lincoln organized his later life around saving the Union, confusion gave way to inner harmony. Some things once important to him now hardly counted at all. Secretary Stanton's harsh and bitter criticism of the President seemed a rather unimportant matter. Lincoln sought to do the will of the Almighty. Then Stanton's willfulness bothered him very little. Lincoln's arrangement of all the elements of his life around his one basic purpose made him great.

Wilberforce of England arranged all his ambitions around the abolition of slavery. Even intense persecution then didn't matter.

Florence Nightingale's unrelenting intention was to nurse the wounded. Hardships were hers that are almost unimaginable to us, now that the nursing profession is accepted and honored. But she was not defeated by difficulties, or upset by them. They were made to take their place of surrender at the feet of her compassionate ministrations to the victims of the Crimean War.

Organization of all that we have and are around a worthwhile goal is the sure way to gain mastery over confusion and victory over petty irritations. What is really important to me? What is my true goal in life? Where, and on what, should I spend my energies?

How would I answer these questions? When I look at the irritations, hurts, and grievances of this week, how much do they really matter? Is it so very important that my husband doesn't answer my questions while he's intent on reading the newspaper? Will it hinder my reaching my life's purpose because my wife is ten minutes late in dressing for the banquet? Will I fail in living a good life because Susan spilled catsup on the tablecloth and Junior ripped his Sunday trousers? Am I utterly done in, totally defeated, because Mrs. Snobbish snubbed me on Main Street? Or will I survive? Have I been spending my emotions out of all proportion to the importance of the stimulus?

Perhaps we are happy at a musical concert because life there is as it should always be. There is a dominant theme and all the other notes are arranged around that theme. Joy is found in nature, because nature is the realm of organization and order. So happiness is found in a life when all of the ambitions, desires, instincts — everything we are, and everything we have — are put together around a central theme. And the only theme big enough to compose a masterpiece of harmony is God.

19

Making Habit Your Friend

An animal's habits can be its undoing. Hunters know this and take ready advantage of the tendency wild creatures have of regularly eating at a certain time of the day and always resting at a particular time or place. Huntsmen are aware that a fox has a definite circuit he follows in his travels. They aim to be nearby when next he passes and ambush the poor fellow. Clever as he is, a red fox can be caught or trapped, most easily by a hunter who knows his habits and lets them lead to his demise.

Personally, I'm not fond of either trapping or shooting foxes. I would far rather melt into the deep shadows of a forest's edge and watch a bronze-red sheen of fur, with brush held high, emerge from a wooded hill and steal on soundless feet across a pasture, searching for meadow-mice and rabbits. But always when I am treated to the sight of a wild animal so engaged in his habitual round of feeding and resting, chasing prey, or eluding predators that he is unaware of my nearness, I am conscious, too, that another watcher, armed and seeking a victim rather than a view, might readily make the animal's habits work his ruin.

Grouse and wild turkey hunters seek out the places where their game habitually feeds. Deer hunters watch the trails regularly used by their prey as they pass from feeding grounds to resting places. Big game men take advantage of the Kodiak bear's practice of sweeping salmon from Alaskan rivers and devouring them. There the hunters wait and the giant bears fall, martyrs of habituation.

Humans are as apt to be ambushed by their habits as are any other creatures. Sir Walter Scott, when a boy, aspired to be at the head of his class in school. But another youngster held that coveted position, and no amount of study or contriv-

- KOHN -

ing seemed to help the future author storm that scholastic stronghold. The opposition held on stubbornly. Then one day young Walter discovered his opponent's weakness. The bright young fellow had a habit that might possibly bring about his downfall. Whenever the lad was called upon for answering questions, he always recited while fumbling with a certain button on his waistcoat. A demonic plot formed in little Walter's fertile mind.

A few days later, Walter Scott appeared in class far more self-confident than usual. His head was light and giddy from breathing the air of imminent success. Within the day, he was sure, he would be the top scholar of his class. Time for recitation arrived. The boy at the head of the class was called upon. As the teacher announced the questions, the boy reached for his waistcoat button. But there was no magical fumbling ritual that day, and no easy spilling of the right answers. The friendly, confidence-inspiring button was gone, and with it his presence of mind! The scholar groped for ideas and words, but they were nowhere to be found. Walter, seeing his long-hoped-for opportunity, answered the questions, snatched first place in his class, and held it throughout the school year.

Later in life Sir Walter Scott, then a world-renowned writer, related the incident, adding, "I have often met him since we entered the world and never without feeling my conscience reproach me. I frequently resolved to make him some amends by rendering him a service, but no opportunity presented itself, and I fear I did not seek one with the same ardor with which I sought to supplant him at school. But this weak little habit of fumbling with the button was his undoing."

Many a person headed for a worthy goal in life has been defeated by a habit. It may be the practice of taking the easiest course of action rather than the soundest one. It might be tardiness, boasting, petty or extreme criticism, inattention to what is going on, nagging, touchiness, intoxication, or narcotics. Cynicism is the mental habit of looking at the worst side of everything. The word "cynic" comes from a Greek word meaning "doglike" — carrying the head down like a dog rather than up like a man. A cynic is one who habitually walks with his nose to the ground, sensitive to stenches, not stars. Whatever the particular practice, there are few tragedies so disheartening as that of a person of high purpose brought low by a bad habit.

Unfortunately, the word "habit" has only a repugnant meaning to most people. When the term is used, a bad habit comes to mind. While it is true that a fox's regular practices may lead to his sudden death from a hunter's bullet or a trapper's snare, it is well to remember that it was habit that kept him alive *until* he was shot — habits of hunting and snatching prey for food that he learned as a cub at the mouth of his mother's den. Habit can be made to work for life as well as death, and for our improvement as well as our collapse.

We gain proficiency in the realm of the spirit much as we do in the province of the physical — by repeated practice. If our vices are habits, so are our virtues. A principle of good living is to find what actions are useful and which ones improve a person's personality and character. Then practice those actions until they become automatic. Cheerfulness is the habit of acting in a hopeful, good-humored way until geniality is automatic. Dependability, tolerance, humility, consideration, tidiness, generosity, and restraint are virtues fashioned by behaving in a right spirit deliberately, often with great effort, and then behaving in that way again and again until one need not ask himself how he will behave *this* time. At last, right behavior is one's natural behavior.

Staying away from church is a habit. So is going to church. The fact that "church attendance is a habit," as some non-church-goers protest, need not prevent one from getting good from worship any more than eating dinner regularly at 6 p.m. need prevent digestion and assimilation. Automatic church attendance, like automatically going to work, or regular meals, or a set time of arising, is a sound and wise habit, sparing you the involved problem of weighing whether or not it should be done *this* time. There is one area of life removed from the tension of indecision or wrong decision.

Rodin, when a struggling sculptor, often became profoundly discouraged. He frequently had a vision of a lovely carving he felt he must bring into being. But he couldn't chisel it into marble. When faced with such frustration, he would lay down his tools, brush the marble dust from his garments, and go to the Louvre. There he would spend a while among the statues fashioned centuries before by the great Greek sculptors. Looking at their classic simplicity and symmetry and pondering on their perfection, he would say to himself, "It can be done, because it has been done. There it is." Then he would return to his studio refreshed, with a renewed faith. And with that new inspiration he used the old tools in the old studio in a new way. Worship does a similar thing for us: it lifts our eyes beyond our failures to Christ. We see in Him life as it should be lived, and we feel "It can be done, because it has been done." We return to the old circumstances with a renewed faith and purpose. Then we do a Christlike deed, although it is most difficult. Later we do a Christlike thing saying, "Well, I did it once before." And at last we do a Christlike thing because we have done it repeatedly and it is automatic. We have made a habit of Christlike behavior.

Good character is little more than a system of well-established good habits. One of the soundest principles for great living is to look for the best; then make the very best your habit. The more you behave in the best possible way, the harder it will become to behave in any other way.

20

Setting the Hook

A good many prize fish are lost simply because the fisherman does not know when to set the hook. He has all the proper gear, a fine boat, the best of motors, the most inviting lures. He casts with infinite skill and finesse. And the huge lunker of a wise old large-mouth bass lunges out from under his sun-umbrella of a lilypad and mouths the bait. The prick of the barbed hook gives him a second thought. With a disdainful air he spits out the bait, whirls, and darts back to his shaded rest beneath the water lilies.

There was a fragment of a moment, a bare split second, when that denizen of the deep was vulnerable. He could have been caught on the barb, played on the line until he was tired and then netted. There would have been envious gasps from covetous fellow-fishermen on the docks, and weighing ceremonies in the cabin kitchen with all the neighbors looking on — if the fisherman had only known when to set the hook.

Harold F. Blaisdell, outstanding authority on game fishing, has said that you can hook more big bass by setting the hook the instant they grab the bait. Hit them with a short line, a taut line, and the bass won't have time to feel the bait, sense the presence of the hook, get wise and in disgust spit it out among the weeds.

Knowing when to set the hook applies to many more areas of life than fishing.

Every successful business man has learned how to make quick decisions. One teacher, lecturer, and writer in business and job efficiency, Dr. Donald A. Laird, has carefully studied the lives of the world's great leaders in business and industry. He insists that "indecision is inaction" and a quick decision is more apt to be right than one we let simmer for a while. The longer a person debates a matter pro and con, the more one's hidden biases and secret prejudices have a chance to work on the issue.

Is there danger of "setting the hook" into the wrong kind of fish, making a mistake through haste? Of course there is! But making a bad choice, in non-moral matters at least, is better than making no choice at all and getting nothing at all. Thomas H. Huxley, eminent scientist of the last century, put it this way: "Next to being right, the best of all things is to be clearly and definitely wrong, because you will come out somewhere. If you go buzzing about between right and wrong, vibrating and fluctuating, you come out nowhere; but if you are absolutely and thoroughly wrong, you must have the good fortune of knocking against a fact that sets you all straight again." In other words, when you feel the tug on your line, set the hook!

Some people can never decide what they want to eat until they wear out the patience of the waiter and all who dine with them. Some women take so long in choosing the dress they will wear to an evening's outing that by the time the choice is made, the occasion is over. Many a man cannot bring himself to a decision as to which necktie to wear to the office. (Solution: own only one tie!) Such folks go through life with their stringers and creels empty because they can never say, "Now is the time! Now I'll set the hook."

Saddest of all cases are those well-meaning people who narrowly miss capturing a far better life because they don't know when to set the hook. They know where the good lies. They see it in church, in the Bible, in the lives of those they admire. They cast a hope or a wish in the direction of a life of service or consecration, clean living or Christlikeness. There's a sudden pull, a tug, something's taken the bait. And then hesitation, indecision — and a slack line. An empty creel and nothing on the stringer.

You know what I mean. You have a generous impulse, but you do nothing about it, and the impulse is soon gone.

You feel like cheering that neighbor, but tomorrow will do. But tomorrow you don't even feel like it.

You could say "Yes" to God now, instead of "Wait a while."

Many an issue would be forever settled that now is a point of conflict in your spirit.

One of the chief secrets of fishing for life's prize catches is in knowing when to set the hook.

21

Rough Edges

It is no great job to collect fireplace wood along the forest's edge this winter. Fallen limbs and toppled trees lie everywhere, making soft mounds in the snow. With help of axe and saw and sled the dead wood is cut into handy lengths and hauled to the cabin. There, while winter howls about the corners of the house and with icy knuckles raps upon the windows, a dozing fire, heedless of winter's commotion, will dreamily nod, grunting in sleepy comfort. Much of the glory of winter is found in gathering wood and burning it in an ample fireplace.

We would seldom have to touch a thriving, growing tree on our acreage in order to have fireplace provender. In this heavily wooded area there are enough dead and dying trees to satisfy the fire's vast hunger. Sometimes, when picking up fuel from the forest floor, my pleasure is blighted to a wee degree by an awareness that I am profiting by Nature's oversight in not dressing the injuries of her long-limbed, high-crowned children. Many a tree is ravaged by disease and dies because when a limb falls under the snow's great weight or is broken by whipping winds, the wound receives no attention. It is then attacked by insects and disease. Often a damaged tree could be saved if the rough edges of its wounds were trimmed away. But Nature does little such trimming, and in the wilderness man does none, and the trees are left vulnerable to insects, disease, and death.

Few secrets of successful living are more important than this: take care of the rough edges. It is there that we are most exposed to diseases that eat away at personality, character and happiness.

Before a little domestic quarrel becomes an infected wound and heart-deep bitterness and decay set in, take care of the rough edges.

Before a slight misunderstanding with an acquaintance or friend can become a big one, take care of the rough edges.

Before single, conquerable mistakes become unconquerable habits, take care of the rough edges.

Before petty pretensions become major hypocrisies, take care of the rough edges.

Before trifling selfishness becomes gaping greediness, take care of the rough edges.

Before fault-finding becomes quarrelsomeness and scolding, take care of the rough edges. It doesn't take long for occasional fault-finding to become nagging. When you first find yourself looking for faults in others and experiencing pleasure in criticisms, beware. Ask yourself *why* you disparage others so heartily. Is it because you feel small and want to cut others down to your size? Is it the fear that others have something you lack, and you turn away from your inadequacies to see if others don't possess worse deficiencies than your own? When you point a finger of accusation at another, the remaining three fingers point backward, at yourself. Try it and see. Now, take care of those rough edges.

Before an occasional disobedience to the known will of God becomes a pervading indifference to God, take care of the rough edges.

Aldous Huxley once told how, when he did something foolish or wrong, he would draw up a genealogy of the blunder. He knew the mistake had a family tree, and he would search for it. What were its parents and ancestors? What would its descendants be like, in Huxley's life and in the lives of others?

Every big blunder and every gross sin has a history, an origin in some small and neglected failure. And all little, overlooked wrongdoings will grow and spread.

Like trees of the Northland we shall all be laden with wintry burdens, and all shall be whipped by heavy winds, and like trees that lose twigs and branches, we shall all be marred. But the injuries need not be fatal. We can keep on thriving and growing if the damage is mended, the rough edges are trimmed and the scars are allowed to heal. Take care of the rough edges.

22

When Conditions Are Right

Every living thing depends upon certain conditions, and none can survive where those conditions do not exist. White-tail deer are browsers, their diet consisting mainly of twigs and shoots of shrubs and trees, of some weeds and a few grasses, of acorns and some fruits. Where these can be plentifully found in North America, one is apt to see whitetail deer. Where these foods are missing, whitetail deer will be absent, as on the American desert or high in the Rocky Mountains. And where the whitetail's diet is present, but meager, the deer do not thrive.

A few years ago a thorough study of the effects of over-crowding in the deer population was made by New York biologists. These scientists compared the breeding status of deer in New York's Adirondack region with that of deer in the southern part of the state. In the Adirondacks, winter piles the snow high upon the slopes, inviting thousands of New Yorkers to the area for bob-sledding and skiing. Many deer, being man-shy, are crowded out of the area. Again, because of the deep snow there, they restrict their movements to small yarding areas where they soon overbrowse the shrubs and trees and then become malnourished. Many starve.

In the southern agricultural counties of the state, which the whitetails have invaded in the past two or three decades, hunting pressure is high, the hunting seasons allow the killing of both sexes, the deer herd has been somewhat thinned out, and food is plentiful.

When game biologists collected a number of does from both of these regions and compared their fecundity, they found some astonishing facts. In the northern overcrowded counties, seventy-eight per cent of the does carried young, while in the southern zone ninety-two per cent were with fawn. About four per cent of the northern doe fawns had bred the first fall season, but

more than thirty-three per cent of the doe fawns of the southern area had bred. In the unfavorable Adirondack area eighteen per cent of the does had twins and only one had triplets. But in the southern agricultural area sixty per cent had twins and seven per cent had triplets.

It is not at all unusual in this Charlevoix area to see twin fawns of the whitetail deer, and upon occasion I have seen triplets. Twins have peered at us over the tall fronds of bracken as we have driven up Hidden Brook lane, and triplets have daintily sipped from our brook and raced upon spindly legs through our orchard.

Multiple births of whitetails in Charlevoix County reveal something about the nature of the wildlife habitat here. Food is plentiful and the deer population is uncrowded. We can know that much from the evidence of multiple births, for fecundity can only occur where the conditions are right for it.

What is true of whitetail deer is so of all other creatures. The muskrat lives and thrives where it can find shallow water for its home and marsh plants and shellfish for its food. Where they are scarce, so are muskrats. Ponderosa pines do well in moist regions of the West, but have not succeeded in crossing the dry, windy Great Plains. Their seeds have been spread far and wide, but almost everywhere they go, aside from their Western habitat, they fail to prosper. Why do we not have alligators in abundance in northern Michigan where water for their frolicking is so plentiful? Because the scaly monsters demand warm water such as is found in the lazy, sluggish rivers of the South. Being cold-blooded creatures, with their bodies taking the temperature of their surroundings, alligators would find their body processes slowed to a crawl in northern waters and they would be in a continuous state of torpor.

Modern medicine has taken advantage of this tendency of living things to live under limiting conditions. Doctors know that bacteria require certain conditions for staying alive. They then proceed to change those conditions, making survival for those bacteria impossible. Many live longest and thrive best in moist, warm, dark places where special chemical conditions are present. Some are killed by being dried out. Others die when heated to high temperature. Some perish from freezing. Many suffer death by exposure to sunlight and fresh air.

One of the most valuable clues nature offers us concerning the successful handling of life is this: if you want the good things in your life to prosper, establish the conditions upon which they thrive. If you want to remove an evil from your life, upset the conditions upon which that evil has prospered.

Faith flourishes when immersed in things that cannot easily be shaken. It falters and dies when grounded in perishables. Some years ago the night sky erupted with an explosion of "falling stars," and in a Negro settlement there were thoughts of impending doom and cries of terror. Several Negroes ran to a white-haired old saint of their race to ask him what they could do. They found the old gentleman on the porch of his rickety cabin with his chair tipped back against the wall, his eyes on the stars and his face alight with smiles. Before they could ask his advice, he ventured. "Ain't dat a pretty sight? Jes see dem little-bitty stars shootin' acrost de sky! But look at dem big ones; dey ain't moved an inch." His faith in the changeless kept him steady.

Fear thrives on inaction. It shrivels and fades when a person acts as if the best were sure to happen. Many a person who has been afraid of flying, when forced by circumstances to take an airplane trip, has come to prefer this mode of travel to any other. Had he never flown, he would have remained fearful. Action made the difference. Most who love diving from a high board were fearful of the first plunge. Action killed the germ of fear. Nearly every famed public speaker admits he was once panicked by the prospect of appearing before an audience. Doing the worth-while thing we fear is like boiling a germ-laden utensil. We create a condition under which fear-germs cannot thrive.

All the good in the world and all the evil depend alike upon the right conditions for their existence and prosperity.

23

The Best Things Cannot Be Hurried*

One reason a solitary saunter over Northland acres brings peace of mind is that Nature has a slower pace than man. When a person leaves a world of crowded places and crowded schedules and walks among the slow-growing trees and the silent hills that seem always to stand at ease, one absorbs a little of Nature's patience. Tranquillity trickles down from the spring-wet boughs of ancient, wind-twisted, time-eroded trees. Calmness oozes up into the stroller from the good old earth that has coolly witnessed the coming and going of ice ages, the deposit and erosion of rocks, the fall and decay of tree limbs and leaves, the building and denuding of the soil, the rise and fall of generations of rabbits and deer and men and all their kin. Nature's patience is contagious and I seek frequent exposure, hoping I can "catch it" again.

Phillips Brooks, the magnificent New England preacher, was well-known for his poise and imperturbability. But his intimate friends knew that he sometimes suffered moments of frustration and irritability. Finding him peevishly pacing the floor of his study, a visitor asked, "What is the trouble, Doctor Brooks?" "The trouble is," Brooks answered, "that I'm in a hurry — but God isn't."

I sometimes wonder if that is not one of the chief troubles of our time: we are in a hurry when God is not. And since, whether we like it or not, the cogs of our lives are engaged with the cogs of God's workings, and the gear teeth of God's plans are stronger than our own, when we speed up and God keeps his own slow pace, we strip our gears. We wear out. We fall apart.

*This article appeared, in condensed form, in the December, 1956, issue of *The Reader's Digest* and is reprinted with the permission of the Editors.

We try to speed up the maturing of our children. When a son behaves childishly at the age of five, we ask, "Why don't you act like a big boy?" Any sensible person ought to know the answer to that — because he is *not* a big boy, nor did his Creator intend him to be a big boy at five years of age. Why should he act like an adult, or an adolescent, or a nine-year-old when he is but five? We want our five-year-olds to conduct themselves like adults, not because it is good for them, but because it is convenient for us; not because it is right, but because we are impatient. There is a time when everyone should act like an adult, and that is when he becomes one. There is a time, too, when everyone should behave like a five-year-old, and that is when he is five. We rob our children of their childhood when we hurry them through it at our wicked pace. We cheat ourselves, too, for we miss our chance to see children as children and forego allowing some of their newness, their freshness, their curiosity and wonder and unrestrained joy to rub off on us.

Our impatience prevents the cultivation of great minds and big souls. It is almost impossible to hasten the cultivation of a good life. Assimilation of the good is a slow process. When James Garfield was president of Hiram College in Ohio, he was approached by the father of a boy seeking admission. The father asked Garfield, "Can't you simplify the course? My boy will never take that all in. He should be able to go through by a shorter route."

"Certainly," James Garfield replied. "I believe I can arrange for that. Of course, it all depends upon what you want to make of your boy. When God wants to make an oak tree, He takes a hundred years. When He wants to make a squash, He requires only two months."

Possibly we read too much and think too little. We want to cram our minds with information and we become like trash-littered attics and junk-crammed basements, where nothing stands out, bold and clear, from all the rest. Everything is lost in the clutter. We might better be like art museums where a few of the best thoughts and ideals are hung upon the walls of our minds to be contemplated at length, while their overpowering truth and beauty are allowed to seep down deep into our subconsciousness. Old attics and old museums have this in

113

common: both bear deposits of things saved from the past. But museums save the best, only the very best, and then clear the clutter of mediocrity away so that the best can be seen and appreciated. Selection and study of the best demands discretion and, even more important, I suspect, patience — an unhurried attitude of mind.

Nature furnishes abundant hints that our mad pace is unnatural. The most important things cannot be hurried. The sun will take its good time in rising and setting. You cannot hurry it. The ice on Lake Charlevoix will melt when the air temperature is right. Scream at it, shake your fists at it, demand that it vanish by tomorrow morning at seven, and you will not affect its rate of melting in the least. The springtime forces that dispel lake ice cannot be hastened.

Warblers will arrive from the South on their spring migration when they are ready. I wish they had been here ten days ago so that our visitors from Illinois could have witnessed their dazzling display of colors and heard their cherubic choruses of call notes. But my wishes were unavailing. Migrating warblers cannot be hurried.

Even inventions, over which man apparently exercises total control, seem to come in their own good time, when the time is ripe and the culture is ready for them. Da Vinci sketched plans for flying machines but could go no further, lacking the necessary motor power. He could not, single-handed, hurry aviation. The invention of the airplane had to wait until the slow, sure progress of civilization provided a well-developed engine capable of sustaining flight.

It has often happened that civilization has waited thousands of years for an invention, and then two or more men have contrived the same device within a single year, as was the case with the telescope, the telephone, and photography. Neptune hung far-off in the sky, a sort of shy child in our solar family, and no man knew it was there. Then, in the same year, two astronomers discovered its presence.

The Psalmist uttered a more profound truth than he knew when he said, "The eyes of all wait upon thee: and thou givest them their meat in due season."

There is real peril in a misapplication of the principle of patience: we may become inactive waiters on events, rather than eventful people who help bring the best to pass. Patience is not passiveness, waiting for everything to be done for us. It is rather the principle of beginning early and taking one's time — or God's time — in getting things done. It might best be illustrated by the young girl who said to her mother just after a white-haired visitor had left their home, "If I could be such a nice old lady as she is — so lovely and so sweet — I wouldn't mind growing old."

"Well, Mary," her mother answered, "If you want to be that kind of old lady, you'd better begin right now. She didn't become a lady in a hurry."

The *best* things cannot be hurried.

24

Simplicity

One of the reasons I love winter in the North country is that this season is one of stark simplicity. A vast amount of summer detail is swept away and only barest elementals remain. Millions of leaves have fallen and now only the naked outlines of the deciduous trees are seen. Evergreen limbs are so deeply covered that spruces, balsam, and hemlock appear less like complex assemblages of needles, twigs, limbs and trunk than simple pyramids of white and green. Multitudes of fair-weather insects and birds and animals have migrated or are in hiding, and only the hardiest creatures of the North brave winter winds and near-zero temperatures to make their appearance. Winter is like a master artist who severely disciplines himself to paint only what is essential to his theme and so rigidly rules out all that is not needed to portray his thought.

Winter is a white and black picture-parable of something fundamental about the universe — its simplicity. Although there are countless millions of heavenly bodies in the unimaginable stretches of stellar space, and although there are hundreds of thousands of kinds of creeping and crawling, walking and flying creatures that populate the earth, and although the green world of vegetation is represented by multiform varieties of plant life, all this multifariousness has a core of simplicity. Only about one hundred elements are in this universe. Their formulas make up all material things, from your body to the most distant star that flickers at the far edge of infinity. The Creator has tied everything together with a simple chain of unity that has little more than a hundred links.

In his beautifully written book, *Wind, Sand, and Stars*, Antoine de Saint Exupery points his readers to the simple and clean lines of an airplane's fuselage and a ship's keel, and reminds us that man's engineering genius has been employed in achieving greater simplicity of line and form, "In anything at all, perfection is finally attained not when there is no longer anything to add, but when there is no longer anything to take away."

Isn't this idea of perfection contrary to much modern thought and practice? We are accustomed to thinking that life would be just about perfect if we could add more property to our estate, more salary to our incomes, more clothes to our wardrobe, more names to our list of social conquests. And what does our generation get for all its acquisitions but more tension, more headaches, more nervous collapse?

It doesn't take a large number of talents to make a great public servant, nor a long list of virtues to make a saint. See for yourself. List the six people in history whose lives are most significant to you. Now place opposite each name the thing for which those people are known. In almost all cases, each person made but one great, single contribution to his time; at most not more than two or three fundamental services were rendered. Just as more notes can be played on the four strings of a violin than on the eighty-eight keys of a piano, so can more varieties of good come from a simple life than from a complex person.

One of the world's greatest benefactors and perhaps its most neglected saint was the man who invented the wastebasket. His invention should be enshrined in a special, sacred place in every home and shop and office and in every public place, a silent reminder of the necessity of eliminating the complicating entanglement of details that confuse and enfeeble our lives.

One day Luther Burbank took a visitor to his experimental gardens at Sebastopol, California, where a half-million lilies were growing. His visiting friends asked Burbank how he would ever manage to market that many lilies, and the plant wizard replied, "Why, we don't market them. We're culling them. My workmen will go through that half-million lilies, cull the half-dozen best specimens, selecting for length and strength of stem, beauty of perfume, contour of leaf and petal, and vigor of body. When they have selected the half-dozen best lilies out of the half-million, the rest will all be destroyed and turned back into the soil again. That is the simple mathematical process of selecting the best. That's the way we work in our laboratories. We throw away a million flowers to get a single bud and plant."

That is the way we get beautiful flowers and the best kind of character — by eliminating the clutter of the worst and the mediocre and all that is less than the best. Look at your life just now. What can you do without? Petty slights? Old grievances? Trashy reading and small gossip? You can name many dispensables. Junk them. Now what is best in your heart and mind? Reverence? Gratitude? Appreciation? Affection? A desire to serve and make your life count? Now that the culls are thrown away, you can concentrate your efforts on cultivating the best within you to the highest degree of perfection.

Simplification is God's way of working, whether it is done by covering the Northland with snow, or binding all things together with a single short chain of elements, improving a lily or perfecting a character.

25

Hugging the Shore

While walking through our town I often delight in the kind of place it is. Sponged by moist breezes, gently washed by surrounding clean waters, and snuggled down comfortably among motherly hills — Charlevoix is a most wonderfully fortunate town.

Then my thoughts saunter back across the years to the long ago when only red men climbed these hills and dipped paddles in these waters. The sound of fog horn or curfew whistle had never shouted above the whisper of pines and the cries of jays and herring gulls.

Then came the white man to Lake Michigan. Nicolet, Father Jacques Marquette, LaSalle, and others slipped along the shore, their birch-bark vessels paddled by Indian braves.

One can imagine Father Charlevoix, the French Jesuit, on his way down the lake from Mackinac to the fort at St. Joseph in his Indian-guided canoe. Like the slender, sensitive finger of a blind man, his frail craft felt along the shore, touched each bay, probed every tributary (possibly investigating our town's Pine River), gathering impressions of this new land.

How was it that the Americas, so rich in beauty and natural wealth, lay here so long before discovery? For one reason primarily. From time immemorial sailors had hugged their shores, fearful of venturing into the open sea. As long as they cherished the comfortable security of seeing nearby land, great discoveries were impossible. Then the Norsemen became more daring than the rest and set sail far out upon the high seas. And, following the invention of the compass, the sailors of West Central Europe launched westward into the unknown. Beyond the mysterious sea and the imagined terrors at the rim of their world, there lay America the beautiful.

How often we hug the shore and shrink from new discovery! Then time, or fate, or the rush of events (or whatever else we care to call our partial views of God) presses us into shipboard service, and we sail out from our beloved harbors of the familiar upon the dark waters of the unknown. And beyond our limited little horizons we find a new world.

We are anxious and filled with foreboding about the tomorrow. But then the hours move out from the snug haven of today and we are aboard. The strand of the unfamiliar future is reached, and we land. And looking back, how glad we are that we left the opposite shore! Although exploring and settling a new land is no easy chore, how seldom we would go back to the old world if we could!

In prospect we fear responsibilities. Taking a new position, having another child, caring for someone who cannot help himself, incurring indebtedness in order to start up a business — how we would rather hug the shore of our present irresponsibility! Then we launch out upon the new adventure and a different world spreads out before us, still better than the old.

An operation faces us. We dread it. At least our present aches and pains have a familiarity about them. But what lies beyond the anesthetic and the deep sleep? We awaken, and before long the old pains are left far behind, and a new world of relief, free of dread, encompasses us.

Just as the Europeans of a few hundred years ago imagined the Atlantic ended in a distant abyss filled with monsters that would gobble up ship and crew, so we fill our minds with images of possible disasters befalling us out there in the future. But as we sail from yesterday through today and visit at last tomorrow, like Columbus we find our imaginations had played dirty tricks upon us. What lie beyond are not ugly monsters to devour us, but unexplored continents to challenge and thrill us.

God has filled the future with exciting discovery for those who refuse to hug the shore.

26

Wise Old Bird?

Where did the owl get his reputation for being a "wise old bird"? The origin of the myth that the owl possesses rare wisdom is obscure, but it is known that in ancient Rome this big-eyed bird was credited with prophetic capacities. Death was supposedly foretold by owls alighting on a housetop, as if by this gesture the bird were predicting the passing of an inhabitant. Probably the owl was first accounted wise because he looks that way. While most birds have their eyes positioned on the sides of their heads, an owl's eyes are placed like man's, in *front* of the face so that the bird can look directly ahead. Moreover, owls' eyes are impressively big, and when they cast a baleful, penetrating glance at a person and then blink knowingly, the onlooker may imagine more intelligence rests behind them than could possibly be the case.

The owl's fabled wisdom is only feather-deep, and these birds have been known to do foolish things, like the one that silently drifted down from its perch, plunged its sharp talons into a startled, ki-yi-ing sixty-pound collie, and tried to fly off with it. Of course the owl's efforts were fruitless, and not being able to get the frightened animal off the ground, the bird abandoned the project. It was a stupid undertaking for an owl, because even a large great-horned owl when de-feathered is little larger than a good-size rooster and is no match for so heavy a burden as a collie dog.

Wisdom is no matter of mere appearances, of having an owl-like knowing look, or a pair of pince-nez glasses, or a large and impressive library, or a long string of academic degrees. One might possess all of these and still be foolish.

Wisdom is a many-sided virtue.

Wisdom is deep knowledge of your own limitations and your own possibilities.

Wisdom is the patience to allow today's seed to ripen into tomorrow's fruit without digging it up every few hours to see how it is coming along.

Wisdom is the hanging of splendid, inspiring thought-pictures on the walls of the mind.

Wisdom sees the essential unity that lies below our human diversity.

Wisdom is being grateful for what you have when you are tempted to mourn for what you lack.

Wisdom means reflecting on what you are about to say rather than only on what you have said.

Wisdom is doing the best you can with what you have right where you are.

Wisdom is the welcome we extend to opportunity, even when it approaches us in grimy overalls and looks like work.

Wisdom is the refusal to be satisfied with noble sentiments and good goals; it develops the *means* to reach worth-while ends.

Wisdom is the power of discrimination, the ability to see a difference between momentary pleasure and lasting satisfaction, the difference between material possessions as means for living and as goals for living. Wisdom distinguishes between fame and greatness, religion and holiness, raw sex attraction and real love, cost and worth.

Wisdom is mental and spiritual neatness, having a plan of life and keeping everything in its place according to its value. That includes putting God in His place, first place, in our scheme of things.

Wisdom is the honest and courageous facing of life's troubles, knowing that some things we travelers do not desire to meet are sure to come our way. Accident or disease may come. If not, at least old age is on its way. So is death. Why treat them as enemies? They are sojourners here with us. They have a place in life's adventure. And who knows, when we are on familiar terms with them, we may dare to call them "friends."

When the haunting hoot of the great-horned owl floats like a ghost of a sound across our moon-drenched meadow, I think of that bird's big blinking eyes, its wise look, and its sometimes foolish behavior. Wisdom that goes no deeper than mere appearances isn't worth a hoot.

Real wisdom is a way of handling life so as to make the most of the short time the Almighty allows us here.

27

What Will It Grow?

One of the chief glories of the North country is the presence of evergreen trees in great abundance. Hemlock, spruce and balsam, white pine, jack pine and others of their kin adorn the emerald hills, rim the cobalt-colored lakes, shelter birds among their ample boughs and spread a generous shade for drowsy deer. Their highest tips finger the first rays of rising sun and stroke the soft glory of sunset skies when day is done. When evening changes into night they point us to the farthest stars.

It is generally thought that evergreens prosper in the North because conditions here are ideal for them. Botanists say that this is not the reason why they stand here in such splendid profusion. It is not because conditions in the North are ideal for evergreens that these trees flourish here, but because the environment is *unideal* for *other* trees. Shorter summers and longer winters—when moisture is unavailable to the trees, being ice-locked in the soil—make growth difficult for such deciduous trees as maples, elms, hickories, and other hardwoods. Some will grow here, but they seldom compete effectively with softwood evergreens which flourish even under the adversities of long winters and less fertile soil. Evergreen trees make the best of an unideal situation. There are some things that the North cannot grow well, but its glory is in what it *will* grow— towering evergreens.

An architect who helped build a beautiful city in an Arizona desert once said that the architecture of any area is not determined by the materials available in the region, but rather by the materials that are *lacking*. When builders have a wide variety of supplies to choose from there is apt to be a diversity

of construction, and no one distinctive type of architecture will predominate. But where there is a scarcity of some kinds of building goods, the architects are forced to use what is available. Scarcity produces an architectural type. If there is little lumber, stone will do. If there is neither lumber nor stone, bricks will serve the purpose. If bricks are lacking, adobe houses can be built. Imaginative builders make their limitations work to produce beauty.

One wise way of handling life is to refuse to describe your situation in terms of its limitations alone. If your environment will not grow an abundance of hardwood trees, it may grow evergreens. If you cannot live in Florida or California, but must live in Northern Michigan, why describe the North in terms of what it lacks — orange groves, year-round deep-sea fishing, flower gardens in January and bathing in the surf in February? Of course the North Country does not provide these luxuries. But it does afford lush growths of evergreens, some of the world's most beautiful inland lakes and streams, cool breezes in the summer, zestful winter sports, wildlife of wide variety and unending interest.

If you cannot be all you would *like* to be under the conditions that environ you, be all that you *can* be. If you cannot grow a spectacular life there, you can still grow a useful one. If you cannot be President, you can still be a good citizen. If you cannot be a great leader, you can still be a great follower — of the best. You cannot be God and fashion the world after your own heart, but you can be God-like and help to make the world better than it now is.

If the soil of your situation will not grow one thing, it will grow another, and like the evergreens adorning the North country and the distinctive architecture of an Arizona city, even your limitations may produce a splendor uniquely your own.

28

Beginning with Mud

The white water lily is one of the loveliest flowers in all of North America. Resting among long-stemmed, rounded leaves on softly moving water that reflects their beauty, or curtsying and swaying to the hum of orchestral insects, or dancing to the drumming of a grandfather frog, white water lilies are things of beauty.

Yet, the elegant charm of this pure white loveliness rises only from muddy lake, pond, and stream bottoms. Water lilies are rooted in mud.

Whenever I hear people excuse themselves for uselessness because of poor background, a limited environment, an unfavorable start in life or crippling circumstances, I think of the water lily and its unpromising beginnings — starting from mud and developing into pure grace.

I think, too, of the many benefactors of our race whose inauspicious beginnings and continued adversities seemed to doom them to an ineffectual existence, but whose spirits rose above it all to produce some beauty of thought or word or deed.

John Kepler, one of the pioneers of modern astronomy, came from a home where both parents were considered "peculiar" and both later went insane. John was a sickly child, a frail youth, and lived out his mature years as a semi-invalid. His first wife was a quarrelsome nag and his second wife a sullen pouter. John's employer, bachelor King Rudolph of Bohemia, was a near-lunatic, and the learned astronomer suffered mightily from the king's odd behavior and ridiculous demands. In spite of all this, or perhaps because of it, John Kepler became one of the world's most noted scientists, preparing maps of the heavens and accurate tables of the stars by which sailors were to navigate for centuries to come. He laid the foundation for the construction of the modern astronomical telescope, discov-

131

ered the three laws of motion of the planets, explained the actions of the tides, and helped establish the new mathematics of calculus. Judging by his poor start in life no one would have guessed his future fame.

One of the most repulsive looking people of his time was Alexander Pope. His ragged teeth were reminders of an ancient and weathered plank fence with many of the boards missing and the rest broken or rotting. His big bulging eyes were like shelled hard-boiled eggs that had become discolored by age. He was so badly hunchbacked that he had to be laced tightly in stiff canvas before he could stand on his feet. Yet, Alexander Pope wrote poetry valued for the smoothness and sweetness of its versification and for brief and memorable phrasing — poetry that claimed for Pope the chief place in the literature of his day.

Frederic Chopin composed seventeen Polish songs, eleven polonaises, fifty-four mazurkas, as well as ballads, fantasies, waltzes, and preludes while struggling against an ailing body and ebbing time. Because he so often verged upon death, news was frequently circulated that he had passed away, and before he was forty years of age the newspapers several times printed the "news" of his death. His friend, George Sand, addressed him as "My dear corpse," and Chopin once gave this summary of his physicians' reports: "One said I would die; the second said I was about to die; the third said I was already dead." The charm of Chopin's music arose from his suffering.

Dostoievsky, whose novels of profound psychological insight have ranked him high among the world's literary figures, was an epileptic, painfully conscious of his handicap.

Pasteur did much of his most brilliant work, advancing the cause of modern medicine, after sustaining a crippling paralytic stroke.

Mozart wrote great operas and composed his immemorial "Requiem" when heavily oppressed by debt and struggling unavailingly against onslaughts of disease which carried him off at an early age.

The happy poems of Frederic Schiller, including his triumphant "Hymn of Joy," were written amidst physical agony and weakness caused by a serious lung ailment.

The lively, lilting music of the light opera, "H. M. S. Pina-fore," was written by Sir Arthur Sullivan while he was enduring the excruciating tortures of kidney stones.

What could people of two thousand years ago expect of any-one whose background was northern Palestine? Not much. They said of Jesus, "Could any good come out of Nazareth?" Rooted in those circumstances He didn't stand a chance. Or did He?

There are no circumstances so good but that the unwise and unimaginative will use them to their own hurt or destruc-tion. There is no situation so adverse but that the wise and the good will turn it to advantage, and, like a lily rooted in mud, make beauty out of it.

29

How Much Can You Stand?

When we see a deer poised on a river's edge, or chickadees flitting from limb to limb, a ruffed grouse strutting across a forest path or a robin digging worms in our front lawn, we are sometimes envious. We covet their freedom from care, their innocence of problems and wish that we could be as "free as a bird" or as poised as a whitetail buck.

Yet if animals could talk our language, many a creature might reply to our envy in the words of the Negro spiritual "Nobody Knows the Trouble I've Seen." While running at high speed through the woods, deer sometimes meet with accidents. Occasionally one spears himself on a sharp projecting branch and suffers serious wounds. The late great naturalist, Ernest Thompson Seton, reported several records of deer which, when killed and skinned, were found to have in their bodies pieces of wood of considerable size. One hunter while skinning a deer found in its body a piece of fir branch over half an inch thick and more than a foot long. Entering the animal between the fourth and fifth ribs on the right side, the branch had narrowly missed the right lung but pierced the top of the diaphragm at the point of the liver. The end of the branch rested against the underside of the backbone. The wound had thoroughly healed on the outside, and the branch was covered with a growth of skin-like tissue. The deer bore every evidence of health, being fat and furnishing excellent meat.

Ruffed grouse, while being prepared for the oven, have shown evidence of meeting with accidents that would seem fatal. Yet they had survived. Large twigs have been found encased in the membranes of a grouse's body, recording some mid-air crash with tree or shrub. But the flesh of the bird had surrounded and accommodated the foreign substance as this feathered prince of the forest continued to strut and beat his drums, feed and mate, and live a normal grouse life.

A robin used to visit regularly the garden of Dr. M. E. Wigham in New Jersey, and he watched it, fascinated, through his binoculars. It was no ordinary bird. It had a stick about three sixteenths of an inch in diameter thrust through its body, protruding about two inches from the back and projecting an inch from the breast. Still the bird went about its business of living as if nothing were wrong.

How is it that some of our animal friends can meet with such trouble and yet live with poise? How do they stand it? This is their secret: If an unlooked-for and unwanted problem hits them, such as a twig or a branch entering their flesh, and they cannot get rid of it, they build tissue around it, integrating it into their system.

How much trouble can a person bear? How much can you stand? That depends upon what you do with your difficulties. You can treat them as foreign substances, rebelling against them, fighting them day and night, letting them distract you from your work, frustrate your purposes and disturb your sleep. Using such measures, you can't stand much. But if you accept them and absorb them into your way of life, count them as part of the scheme of things, work your plans and purposes around them as a deer or a grouse or a robin builds living tissue around a twig in its body, you can stand a great deal more than you've ever guessed.

30

Face Into the Storm

Among my foul-weather friends I cherish the black-capped chickadee as one of the most companionable. When the first hints of autumn chill the air, and fair-weather birds flee to more comfortable climes, the chickadee remains. And when I saunter through a cedar clump, reading track-tales of animal adventures of the night before, a chickadee is sure to carol a cherubic welcome. From cedar bough and spruce branch, from balsam twig and birch limb, on the sunniest days and in the most merciless storm of snow or sleet, all winter long the chickadee's cheerful chant rings out.

One reason why the black-capped chickadee can survive hard northern winters is that it has the good sense to face into the wind. Like the feathers of all the birds, a chickadee's feathers lie pointing tailward. If the bird turns its back on winter winds, snow will blow in amidst the feathers, carrying the raw and bitter cold next to the body, where it can nip at the blackcap's warmth and finally freeze it to death. But when a chickadee faces into the wind, snow flurries are stopped by the close matting of its feathers, which hold in body warmth and fend off savage weather. A black-capped chickadee endures the winter by facing the storm.

Many a human disaster is caused by facing away from the wind, seeking to escape reality, ignoring the facts of life. The psychiatrists' offices overflow with people who have thus allowed adversity to ruffle their feathers, penetrate them, and benumb their spirits.

Alcoholism is the result of an attempt to escape the winds of existence by turning the other way, in the direction of illusion. Drug addiction is a similar evasion of reality.

Neurotic invalidism turns one away from responsibilities so that he does not need to serve his generation, but can be waited

upon, ministered to constantly by those unfortunate enough to be attached to him by ties of blood or sympathy. His chief trouble is not organic, but mental, a desire to ignore reality. If the neurotic doesn't receive all the pity or attention he craves, he feels neglected, misunderstood, and mistreated. He feels he is a martyr, and martyrdom is another kind of escape from reality. It makes one feel important, ranked with the saints who have suffered for great causes.

The only people who entirely escape from this world are the dead and insane. Withdrawing from reality, the insane design a little world of their own where they are God, or Napoleon, or the Queen of England and have everything to their liking. They are then hospitalized in institutions for the mentally ill, where they know of no responsibilities and where everything is done for them, food and shelter are provided for them, and they can linger for months or years or a lifetime in a world of fantasy, pretending there are no storms.

Each of us is a limited person and needs to face his limitations courageously. No one can do everything expertly. No matter how good you may be in one area of achievement or how you might excel everyone you know in another endeavor, someone near you can surpass you in still some other undertaking. Why be jealous? Why stand by, glowering, contemptuous, begrudging another his success? Let's face it, you cannot be supreme in everything.

The person who stays spiritually healthy through life's worst storms is one who faces them. He is prepared for all weathers that come, knowing they are all a part of normal human experience and all serve some purpose. He knows there is nothing that need utterly destroy him, nothing at all — temptation, responsibility, failure, pain, bereavement, or death. His happiness is in the conviction that his Creator has outfitted him with an inner warmth and an outer covering that defy the chill of any wintry storm if he will only face into the wind.

31

What the Storms Reveal

As the sun slowly slipped beneath the horizon on a stormy evening a few days ago, angry white waves charged across Lake Charlevoix and broke upon the rocks just below our house. All night the pounding of the waters continued, and the next morning we heard a seething and a sighing as the lake panted from its futile efforts to destroy the shore.

Then, as the faint light of sunrise was reflected from one cloud bank to another all across the sky, water birds began to gather just off-shore to breakfast upon the repast the waves had inadvertently delivered at our beach. American golden-eye ducks, on their fall journey toward coastal waters, came for aquatic insects, crayfish, and shrimplike crustacea the storm had wrested from the lake bottom and deposited in the shallows along the shore. Merganser ducks dipped together, as if at a signal, to catch minnows the storm-tossed waves had corraled among the off-shore rocks. Herring gulls wheeled and dove with uncanny accuracy, quickly coming to the surface with trapped and hapless minnows struggling in their beaks. A tempest before which once the birds had fled had now spread a bounteous banquet before them.

Life's adventure is somewhat like a Lake Charlevoix storm is to the birds. We flee from a tempest. Naturally we do. But when the tumult is over, we discover that it has produced good as well as havoc and something upon which the hungry soul can feed.

A long illness often brings to our attention a tenderness in loved ones and friends, in nurses and doctors, in women who clean hospital wards and orderlies who perform menial services —a tenderness that was hidden from us until trouble brought it out.

How often a bereaved person, still suffering shock from a sudden loss, exclaims, "I never realized I had so many friends until now!" People whom we know only as acquaintances now show up as friends. They were friends all along but it took sorrow to reveal them for what they were.

Often we are ungrateful for the many public servants who unobtrusively work for our welfare until some disaster demonstrates how much they are needed and what they have meant to us. Mrs. Mildred S. of Pittsburgh, Pennsylvania, thought little of the traffic policeman's importance until her son was killed on a dangerous street corner. Then she applied for the position of a traffic policewoman, explaining, "If I could help prevent one accident, I know the pain I could spare a mother." Trouble had dislodged some remote and unrecognized appreciation in her spirit and had floated it into the forefront of her mind.

Our own spiritual resources seem feeble. When we see suffering in prospect, we exclaim, "I don't think I can stand it!" But when trouble comes, we do endure it, bearing it better than we could have guessed. A mother who is devoted to her family and particular about her housework gets bone-tired and so depleted she feels as if the necessity of lifting her little finger would make her drop in complete exhaustion. Then her baby falls ill and the infant's need releases resources within her that keep her going through sleepless nights for weeks on end.

A missionary to the Philippines has related how, when the missionaries were ordered into prison camp during World War II, they were told they could take with them only what they could carry in their suitcases. His wife, who was not at all strong and weighed a mere 105 pounds, toted a load of 200 pounds four and a half miles. Upon arrival at the prison neither the missionary nor his wife could lift the load from the ground. One scientist has reported that we normally employ about one-eighth of our physical powers. We do not know how much strength we have until a crisis demands it. So with our spiritual resources. They are more plentiful than we have guessed.

Deep within us God has hidden reserves of which we are unaware until some storm of the spirit dislodges them, and they break loose from their hiding places and are made available for our use.

32

The Friendly Dark

The setting sun has bathed the western sky with splendor. Twilight has mellowed and darkened the vivid flush, and now that the sun has dipped the required eighteen degrees below the horizon, night has come.

Some moments ago a ruffed grouse hen completed an evening meal of beechnuts and buds. Then, having quenched her thirst at the nearby brook, she lifted her head skyward, chose a rugged, twisted branch on a nearby maple and there settled down for the night. Darkness came, and with the blackness of the night there settled upon this gamy denizen of the forest a deep peace akin to trust. No marauding fox could see her now, or reach her. Nightfall silenced the thundering guns of hunters and the menacing prowling of their dogs. Goshawks, those bloodthirsty pirates of the air, put to port at day's end and must await dawn before plunging their talons into the flesh of more ruffed grouse. Melted into the shadows and shielded by surrounding limbs, the hen is safe, too, from the clutches of the horned owl. She rests. She stirs slightly and then becomes still again. The alert eyes close, and she falls to sleep sheltered by the friendly dark.

Beneath her scamper the gem-eyed mice, white feet leaving a delicate embroidery of elfin tracks on the dust of fallen leaves. Most of the day they tremble in fear of their many enemies — foxes, hawks, butcher birds, prowling cats from neighboring farms, skunks, shrews, snakes, and a host of other predators. Almost every meat-eater is eager for a meal of deer-mouse, and all day long the furtive little fellows huddle in hiding from their furred and feathered enemies. Then darkness comes. From thousands of sheltered haunts the deer-mice scurry to satisfy their hunger. They are daring now, guarded by the friendly darkness.

143

Deer, too, are about, especially if the forest glades are silvered with moonlight. They browse. They drink from the laughing water of a favorite stream. Darkness drives many an ancient dread away and proffers a new freedom of movement to the whitetail deer.

Small birds await the night for migration, some primitive and vague awareness whispering to them that darkness is their friend to guard them from their foes.

Darkness is even more an expression of nature than is light. The distant burning suns and stars are but glittering sequins on nature's dress of midnight blue. The vast background is dark; the tiny sparkles are light. The surface of the sea twinkles with reflected sunshine falling upon the many-faceted waves. But below two thousand feet no light penetrates, and all is blackness. Yet life is there in the stygian depths. Queer-looking fish dart about. Arrow worms troop up and down the dark corridors of the wrinkled sea floor. Strange phosphorescent shrimps live their entire lives without ever seeing a ray of light. The vast ranges of the sea are dark. Only the surface is light. Yet the darkness is cordial to life, welcoming it, sheltering it, and supporting it.

We often speak of our troubled days as "dark days." But look back over the years. With your imagination pry up, lift out of your life and discard all the dark times you have known, all of your troubles. Throw away, too, the good your troubles have germinated and grown in you — patience, courage, persistence, faith in God. What would you have left? Not much of a person!

The darkness as well as the light has nurtured you. Some virtues have thrived in the long shadows of your night that would never have survived the constant glare of perpetual sunshine.

Darkness can be a friendly thing.

33

One Secret of a Happy Life

The excessive timidity of the cottontail rabbit fascinates me. I've sometimes wondered why, and I've just about concluded that it is because the rabbit's chronic anxiety is so closely paralleled by a similar fearfulness often found in human beings. The rabbit is a victim of *indiscriminate* anxiety. Unlike the common crow of North America, which seems to detect the difference between a man carrying a walking stick and one holding a gun and will act boldly toward the first and flap away, scolding harshly, from the second, the cottontail runs as fast from the one as from the other. The cottontail bounces away from the hunter who carries a gun and aims to take his life. But he also flees from the most innocent, unarmed nature lover who is merely out for a casual saunter and would do him no harm. The bunny imagines harm where there is none. He suffers from a morbid imagination.

A timid person is like an anxious rabbit, scourged by fancied evil all around him. And there is no timidity or morbid imagination worse than that caused by hidden guilt feelings.

The guilty fancies evil where none abides. He dreams up motives in the minds of others that are unreal. He is plagued by enemies that are non-existent. As the writer of Proverbs said: "The wicked flee when no man pursueth."

The person who has committed a crime and is as yet uncaught is afraid of all representatives of the law. Not only the policeman on his track frightens him, but *all* policemen are regarded as his enemies.

A woman whose misdeeds have thus far been successfully hidden is afraid of all whispering. She not only fears the whispering that is about her, but all whispering, because it *might* be about her.

A man who has violated his marriage vows and has been disloyal to love is apt to resent all his wife's questioning about his whereabouts. No matter how innocent the inquiry may be, he fears it signifies she may know something about his unfaithfulness.

The business man or woman who has been disloyal to a trust in handling someone else's money is chronically fearful that people know. The most harmless questions concerning his stewardship strike terror within him. Has anyone guessed? Does someone know? Are they catching on?

There are some people who could never feel comfortable in church, because whenever the Bible is read it speaks of their condition. It finds them. Whenever a sermon of profound insight into human nature and human need is preached, they feel as if their condition is known. They can't quite put their finger on the cause, they will tell you, but going to church — any good church — makes them feel uneasy.

In the Old Testament book of Genesis the story is told of how Adam and Eve had eaten the forbidden fruit. Then they hid themselves away in the garden, attempting to escape God's sight. But God called out for Adam, asked him where he was and why he was hiding, and Adam answered, "I was afraid . . . and I hid myself."

That is the story of guilt in Old Testament days and in all time. Guilt feelings make a man shrink from discovery. He becomes fearful and furtive.

As the old Roman, Publius Syrus, put it, "A guilty conscience never feels secure." And Shakespeare later added, "Conscience doth make cowards of us all."

There is only one satisfying answer to such guilt-induced timidity. The cure is forgiveness. Confession should be made to the person aggrieved whenever that is possible. It often helps to tell a wise counselor. Above all, God should be told of our penitence, even though He already knows, and He should be asked for forgiveness, for all wrongdoing at long last is against Him. Restitution should be performed, and then, when secretiveness is at an end, one will not feel furtive, for there will be nothing to hide.

No spiritual urge is greater than this need to be forgiven. Nothing else matters much until that is done, and a person can stand almost anything as long as his conscience is clear and his heart is clean. Dr. Roy Burkhart once told about a boy who left home to do something that his parents felt was morally wrong. While gone, he was involved in an accident and lost both legs. The boy was broken-hearted, and so were his parents when word of the tragedy reached them. In telling the story later, the boy's father said, "When his mother and I saw him in the hospital cot, lying there aware that he had lost both legs, he said, 'Will you forgive me?' We both hugged him and said, 'Of course. We have already forgiven you.' Then the boy exclaimed, 'Then I can live without my legs!'"

A person can live happily without legs or arms or hearing or sight, as hundreds of handicapped persons have proved. But no one can be happy with an uneasy conscience.

One secret of successful and happy living is that of having a clear conscience.

34

Making Room for Others

Trees and shrubs are budding now, and soon the Northland, for so many months a study in the somber tones of winter, will be alive with vivid greens.

Creamy white birches are clothed with a film of yellow-green as are their cousins, the poplars. From a distance many of the hardwoods' infant leaves seem to be antiqued with a faint bronze cast, as if a rich golden brown tint had been painted over the underlying green and then wiped off.

Throughout the eastern half of the United States the flowering dogwood spreads its tiers of white, pink-tinged bracts above the woodland floor, and soon throughout the continent our most prized fruit trees will flower forth in delicately colored spring gowns.

Amidst all of this rampant budding, blossoming, and leafing out, it is a wonder to me that leaves and flowers on the same tree do not overcrowd each other. Yet this seldom happens, as if there were an innate thoughtfulness and courtesy at work in nature. An experiment worth trying in springtime or summer is to take a leafed-out twig of almost any shrub or a cutting of nearly any plant and twist it around in your fingers. See how many complete turns of the stem are necessary before a leaf springs forth from the stem directly above any of the leaves arranged below it. Leaves do not burst from a stem haphazardly or in an accidental order. They are so placed on the stem as to make room for each other, so that each gets its share of sunshine and rain.

Wouldn't this be a much better world if all of us learned the lesson of a leafing plant and so lived our lives that each of us overshadowed others as little as possible?

35

From an Elevation

Nearly all songbirds carol their characteristic songs while in flight or while perched on an elevated object, such as a tree limb, a stump, a telephone wire, or a bush. Those perky, happy-hearted little winter songsters, the black-capped chickadees, chant their joyous songs from woodpiles, sap buckets, balsam boughs, axe handles — anything they can find that lifts them above ground level. Chickadees may occasionally chirp a little while embroidering tracks across the earth's wintry blanket of snow, but they will seldom chime their clear-ringing "chick-a-dee-dee" until a suitable perch is found.

Some birds are content with singing perches only slightly above the surrounding grassland, while others demand considerable altitude. The savannah sparrow requires nothing higher than a hummock a few inches above his surroundings. The robin seems to prefer a high limb, but if one isn't available when the urge to sing seizes him, he will settle for a twig on a sizable bush. But field sparrows, larks, and indigo buntings, which will nest in low locations, require perches for singing that are much higher than their nesting level. Songbirds seek elevation for their singing.

Early in the history of sound motion pictures, a movie producer decided to film and record birds singing in their natural habitats. He thought such a project would demonstrate in a dramatic way the advantages of sound pictures. During the singing season the producer sent two cameramen into good territory with orders to bring back films and sound recordings of a variety of bird songs. After many days of arduous search the cameramen admitted utter defeat. Their days in field and forest had proven fruitless. Not one foot of sound film had they used. Dr. Arthur Allen of Cornell University's ornithology department was approached by the two camera experts and told of their desperate plight. They could hardly face their boss with no bird songs whatsoever. Even a record of one bird's song would help. Dr. Allen told the men to drive their sound truck along a certain country road. He asked them to stop by a particular bush and set up their equipment. Then he suggested that they focus their apparatus on the top of the bush and they would get a splendid recording of a song sparrow's voice.

The cameramen were skeptical, since there wasn't a bird within sight or hearing, but they followed Dr. Allen's instructions. And soon, as the men became settled in position and quiet, a male song sparrow flew up to his choicest singing perch and chanted a cheery song. Dr. Allen knew where and when a song sparrow was apt to sing. Feathered songsters need a certain height from which to express their spirits.

Normal people do too. They need some elevation before their spirits burst forth in song. The pathological may find a kind of contentment in a low life, as the kleptomaniac is restless until he steals, and the pyromaniac until he starts a destructive fire. In low perversity the abnormal mind finds a satisfaction akin to joy. But we recognize such behavior and such people as "unnatural." By nature we are fitted for singing from elevations.

When do we feel most like singing? Isn't it when we have arisen to some height above life's ground level, above our average performance? We are in a singing mood when we are giving more than we are getting. Songs come to mind and heart and lips when we are most conscious of God's greatness, His love, and His approval.

Maybe we are happiest at Christmastime because life is then most nearly what it should always be, giving is better than receiving, another's happiness more important than our own, and God seems strangely near. No wonder even folks who "can't carry a tune in a basket" love to carol at Christmas. Christmas is an elevation above ground level, the year's choicest "singing perch."

36

Living on Tiptoe

By the changing parade of budding, blossoming, and fading flowers nature is constantly reminding us that even the most beautiful material things are not meant to last forever. When I visited my favorite brook late yesterday afternoon, the terraced banks had lost their nodding blaze of yellow lady-slippers. Only a few weeks ago they were at their peak of loveliness. A week ago an occasional withered survivor drooped wearily as if having no wish to go on. Now all are gone. But where lady-slippers once flourished, white windflowers now sway on slender stems, the purple member of the mint clan, selfheal, tosses in the breeze, and the low-growing yellow hedge hyssop waves agreeably to every passing gust of wind. So as seasons succeed each other, wild flowers with an elegant politeness bow out of the scene and give place to each other. Marsh marigolds, trilliums, violets, wild columbines and flowering raspberries greet their successors, curtsy, and fade out. The newcomers have their day, salute those who are to follow them, and then depart.

In such a world of change a person must decide how he is to live — mournfully or expectantly. Shall we lament the blossoms that have faded or anticipate with joy the flowering of beauties yet to come?

God never allows a joy to depart but that He has another about to arrive. This is so of the process of aging — infancy, childhood, youth, maturity, and old age each having its peculiar satisfactions which no other season of life can ever know. Enjoy each period as you can, pressing from it all possible good, and then let it pass without regret, awaiting with eagerness the delights of other approaching days.

Marriage too has its buddings, blossomings, and fadings from the bright ardor of honeymoon to the vivid glory of parent-

hood and the more delicately shaded fragrant flowering of tender companionship. Those who mourn a marriage because the intense flush of honeymoon days has passed are fools who love the buds of May but ignore the equally resplendent blossoms of July and September.

And what of the passing of those dear to us? A perennial spirit but fades from our sight for a while, but it will live again to greet our eyes once more with fresh beauty when another season of the soul has come.

The fading of the flowers is as much God's doing as is their blooming. Each has a place in His scheme of things. The mood of faith is not a slouch into despondency but standing on tiptoe to see what new good thing God has in store for us just over the horizon of another day.

37

Little Things

Ordinarily we think we owe America's greatness to explorers and pioneers and settlers. In part we do. They performed prodigious feats of heroism to discover these shores, settle this land, push back our frontiers, and pioneer an American way of life. When we consider America's beginnings, we reflect upon red men and their primitive civilization, the clash of muskets and the silent flight of arrows, the thud of the woodman's axe, and the groans of men and women lifting timbers into place, building lonely log cabins deep in the emerald wilderness. We visualize canoes manned by sun-bronzed huntsmen returning from the kill with provender for another week, and hard-muscled plowmen wrestling wooden plows around white-pine stumps and shouting orders to unhurried oxen.

But besides the valiant performances of early American pioneers, we owe credit for life here and everywhere to a ridiculously small, commonly misunderstood form of life — bacteria. Sounds foolish, doesn't it? But it's true. Those who have studied the nature of our world most thoroughly insist that bacteria are the foundations of life here and everywhere. They have established the base upon which all other forms of life rest.

Say "bacteria" to the average person, and he thinks at once of microscopic, disease-causing creatures that are his worst enemies. To be sure, there are pathogenic forms of bacteria against which medical science is fighting. But the harmful bacteria form about as high a proportion of the entire bacteria population as convicted murderers do among the human population of the United States.

Most bacteria are helpful servants in the natural world. They break down vegetable and animal tissue to make rich soil,

159

without which food crops would be impossible. They are nature's scavengers and janitors, removing the dead and keeping the good earth clean. They break up rock and incorporate it into soil. Bacteria live amidst the roots of plants and help them make use of the nutriments in the soil. They exist in the digestive tracts of animals, including man, softening the hard cellulose of plant food so that it can be digested. There would be no life-supporting soil in America, no sanitation, no plants, no animals, no human beings, if it were not for bacteria which most of us have never seen. While we sing the praises of our founding fathers, we might remember too these infinitesimally small, commonly overlooked, and usually abhorred pioneers of life, the bacteria. The biggest things in America depend, directly or indirectly, on these little things.

In fact, wherever you go in nature or in life, the biggest things depend upon the littlest things. The vitality of a seed lies not in the largest, most obvious part, the meat, but rather in the small, almost imperceptible, embryo. In the seed of the coconut palm this center of vitality weighs only one two-thousandths of the entire weight of the coconut minus its husk. It is the tiniest part of a seed, the embryo, that contains the life of future plants.

One of nature's most powerful levers is a little thing—an ice crystal. A drop of water rolling into a narrow crevice of a rock freezes. The drop becomes a crystal of ice, irresistibly expanding until the rock is split in two. What man does with dynamite and gigantic hammers, nature accomplishes with the smallest wisp of moisture left over from a late fall rain.

Lowly little earthworms benefit the soil, dragging into their burrows dead leaves and other organic material. There they leisurely feed upon it, carelessly leaving scraps of their dinner in their underground dens. These neglected left-overs become mixed with the soil, enriching it. Earthworm tunnels open the soil, allowing water and air to enter freely. Worm castings comprise much of nature's fertilizer.

As we mature in mind and spirit, we lose our proneness to be impressed by mere size. A small child may prefer a nickel to a dime because the nickel is larger. But as the child matures, he learns that largeness is not a sound basis for judging all values. When the youngster at last becomes a parent, he will love his new-born child as much if it weighs but six pounds as if it weighed ten. Love is not a matter of ounces and pounds or measurement from the bottom of pink little feet to the top of a woolly little head. Love recognizes that highest values are beyond physical dimension and that some of our dearest possessions are little ones.

Too much emphasis is placed upon the great, conspicuous deeds of men and not enough on the little, daily acts which make memorable deeds possible. The worst we do and the best are alike traceable to small deeds. Just as a drunkard becomes flagrantly drunk by so many individual swallows of liquor, so we develop good morals and strong character that are obvious in a crisis by many individual little courageous acts. Libertines are not made suddenly. Neither are heroes or saints. By doing difficult things daily and in good spirit we build the resources to face victoriously a rare and monumental problem.

Helen Wills Moody, famed tennis star, once said that she learned to play championship tennis by making each swing of the racket her best.

Mrs. Anne Emery once revealed how she had written her novel *Tradition*. "My routine for ninety days was to snatch fifteen minutes at the typewriter after putting one child to bed or between feedings. I was able to get twenty minutes after sending the two oldest off to school in the morning and another half hour or so while the kids slept after lunch." Charles Dickens reflected such an appreciation of small snatches of time and little doses of opportunity when he said in *David Copperfield,* "Trifles make the sum of life."

Sometimes when I ponder the big consequences of little things, like a ten-word telegram or a casual word of encouragement or a "thank you" note or an encouraging handclasp or a thoughtful, unexpected, and inexpensive gift or a moment's fun and companionship with a little child, I wonder if there is anything more worth while than doing little things.

As some unknown seer has put it, "If you do a small thing as if it were a great thing, God will let you do the great thing as if it were a small thing."

38

Small Things Make Big Differences

Against the somber black and white of the winter landscape we often see a startling blaze of blatant blue where a blue jay darts from limb to limb of woodland trees. Just now, in January, few colorful birds are seen. The brownish English sparrow is here, as is the dusky starling. The gravely dressed crow can be found and the lusterless brown creeper. But the brilliantly garbed tanagers, orioles, and goldfinches have deserted the North for milder climes.

Perhaps the blue jay remains in the Northland because he feels more at home here, having helped to make these woodlands. A nut eater, the blue jay stuffs himself all fall and buries what acorns and beechnuts he cannot eat under sticks and leaves. Then when winter comes and food is harder to find, he digs up his hidden store. But, being a forgetful creature, the bird does not remember where all his cache is hidden. In the spring these forgotten nuts sprout in the damp soil. Some of them grow into trees. Many an oak and beech forest owes its existence in part to a forgetful blue jay.

While pondering over the difference a blue jay makes in the tree population of Michigan, I've been dwelling, too, upon the multitude of other small things that make big differences. Seeds are small things, and the germinating of plants absorbs very little of our total thinking. But supposing that this year everything else went along as usual, much as last year, but with one exception. Just suppose that this year all seeds ceased ripening. Not one seed in all creation would sprout and grow. There would be no grain crop in the entire world, no vegetable harvest, and no new grass growth. Cattle would starve. Human beings would perish. The danger of a hydrogen bomb would seem as harmless as a child's water pistol when compared to the devastation wrought on earth if all seeds remained unsprouted for just this one year. Small things make big differences.

The history of civilization has often been affected by a very small and seemingly insignificant occurrence. Some scholars declare that North America might have been as predominantly Roman Catholic as is Central America had Columbus reached the Western Hemisphere in March instead of October. As he neared the shores of this hemisphere Columbus followed the flocks of migrating birds, sure that they would lead him to land. In October the migration was southward, thus leading Columbus to Central America where he landed and began propagating the Roman Catholic faith. Had he arrived in the West in March, the migrating land birds would have been flying northward, directing Columbus toward North America, where he would have claimed the land for the Roman Church as well as for Spain. The small matter of timing made a big difference.

We frequently hear it said, "People are the same all over the world." The saying is true if it means that all earth's children have pretty much the same basic urges and drives for food and comfort, for mating, for power over things, and for the admiration of fellow human beings. But the little differences have big consequences. All trade is built upon those little differences. Some people like to farm, others prefer fishing, some like mechanics, others prefer sales work, many like the fine arts. If it were not for these little differences in preferences, everyone would want the same job. Diversification, which makes for trade, would be impossible.

The nerve of a tooth is not as large as the finest cambric needle. If it is healthy we are unconscious of its being in our jaw. But if disturbed, such a nerve can drive a strong man nearly out of his mind.

Optic nerves are small things, yet let them be removed and you are without sight. Over these tiny cables of tissue travels all the visual splendor you will ever see. The optic nerve is a small thing that makes a great difference.

A foot is a small measurement, a mere twelve inches, but what a difference it would make if added to the length of your nose!

One short hour spent in inspiring worship on Sunday can make a big difference in the other 167 hours of your week.

The key to your day is your treatment of your first half hour after waking. Spend it grumbling and your day will likely be ruined. Use your first waking moments in grateful realization of the glad gift of life and the opportunities spread before you and your day is blessed.

The secret of handling life's big problems victoriously is to be found in handling the trifles well.

Small things make big differences.

39

Perennial Pleasures

As fall comes on and moves toward winter a marked difference between two kinds of plants becomes apparent. Some plants are dying after a single season of growth. Their species will survive because of seeds the dead plants will leave behind, but the short-lived plants themselves will pass away. These ephemeral members of the vegetable kingdom we call "annuals." Some annuals are killed by frost. Others appear to die of sheer exhaustion, the production of flowers and fruit completely depleting their stores of energy and leaving them without the power to carry on. Then there are the "perennials" which possess the necessary vitality for bearing flower and fruit, surviving frost and winter snows to greet another springtime with blossom and another summer with growth and fruitfulness. Some perennials shed their leaves and seal their buds against winter rigors and withdraw all signs of life within the fortress of their woody stem. Others, like our evergreens, manage to hold their needle-like leaves through the worst freezings and heaviest snows a Northern winter can offer. Still others form bulbs or rhizomes or tubers which shelter and nourish the life of the plant until another growing season arrives. Even the novice gardener knows that there exists a great difference among the plants, some being short-lived annuals and others having a perennial vitality.

Pleasures are like plants. Some are annuals, here for a season, but soon gone. The first frost of adversity kills them, or age withers them, or they may die of sheer exhaustion. But there are perennial pleasures, too, that belong to no single season of the soul but have a built-in lasting quality that sees them safely through many a chilling crisis and past numerous bleak circumstances.

The aging process tests our pleasures and manifests their durability. When the first bloom of life has faded and the raw new energies are gone, what is it then that makes some people enthusiatic, fascinated, and fascinating, as was the famed naturalist, John Burroughs? Although Burroughs was nearly eighty-four years of age when he died in 1921, he was still a youngster at heart. To his family and friends the great student of nature was known as "the boy who never grew up." When eighty he could still squeeze as much enjoyment from a fishing trip as most boys can at eight. If his luck was good, he was as pleased as a barefooted lad with his first string of perch. If his creel remained empty, Burroughs still returned home with an exciting catch of new information about birds or beasts he had seen at the lake's edge, a strange song he had heard from the topmost twig of a towering tree, or some new thought that stirred his mind while his hook and line plumbed the lake's blue depths. John Burroughs' capacity to force every experience to yield its quota of wonder and excitement accounted for his durable youthfulness. Anyone who learns to press the good out of every occasion will find perennial pleasure.

Moreover, perennial pleasure can be found in the enjoyment of things you cannot solely possess. Elbert Hubbard derived much satisfaction from visiting art galleries although he openly confessed he knew little about the fine arts. One time when he was enrapt in the beauties of an oil painting, a friend jokingly asked, "Why do you permit yourself to become so enthusiastic over things you can never afford to own?"

Hubbard replied, "I would rather be able to appreciate things I cannot have than to have things I am not able to appreciate!"

One reason for the restlessness of our times is that our civilization has provided us with too much, so much that we cannot enjoy it at all, and some of the wonders that were here before civilization became so complex we don't take time to appreciate. How long has it been since you spent fifteen consecutive minutes looking up at the stars or at a sunset sky or at an old masterpiece of fine art? Let greedy possessiveness fade from lack of care, and begin cultivating appreciation for those things that are here for all who have open eyes and hearts.

Plant and nourish in the little children who are under your influence pleasure in the wonders of the world around them.

With the best of intentions but with the poorest of techniques we attempt to make our children happy. We lavish upon them gifts and toys. We excuse them from duties around the house. Some toys are necessary for children, and some freedom to do about what they please is important to their welfare, but toys are easily broken, and a youngster cannot be protected from work forever. If we teach a child to seek his satisfaction in gadgets and freedom from duty, we doom him to misery, for there will always be gadgets he cannot afford or of which he will rapidly tire, and life will always thrust upon him responsibilities that must be borne.

But stimulate a child's growth and spur his development so that he constantly seeks information that will broaden his mind and experiences that enlarge his spirit, and enduring happiness will be his. Encourage his wonder at life's mysteries. Many parents are prone to discourage wonder rather than to promote its growth. John H. Crowe has reported how a little girl on a train trip with her mother kept looking out the window and shouting, "Look, Mama, a horse," and, "Look, a cow!" After some time the embarrassed mother apologetically explained to other passengers sitting near, "You know, she still thinks everything is wonderful." At sixty or eighty that girl can still think everything is exciting and marvelous if the tender plant of awe is not uprooted by a careless parent, for wonder is one of life's perennial pleasures.

Again, lasting enjoyment can be found, if we will look for it, in essentials rather than superficialities. A fisherman watched an overdressed summer visitor mince down the street of a resort town, and muttered to a friend, "I reckon the riggin's worth more than the hull." In many cases it is. We have invested more money in vehicles and less pleasure in travel than any nation in history. We spend more money on houses and less time in our homes than any modern people elsewhere in our world. Our generation places more stress on appearances and less on moral health than any generation has for several centuries. We are a people interested in piecemeal self-improvement. What cannot be accomplished by a change in shade of face powder or by using a different brand of tooth polish may be achieved by reading book condensations. We get inoculated with small doses of religion in order to keep us

169

from catching the real thing. We buy the prettiest clocks and have the least time for enjoyment of silence, solitude, blue skies, country lanes, kind looks, leisurely contemplation, and the company of a friend than have any people in the annals of the human race. And it's all because we have forgotten what counts most.

A little girl of kindergarten age one day came home from school with a kitten she had found wandering in the alley. She loved it as only a little girl can love a newly discovered kitten, and the kitten responded to her affection wholeheartedly. They were almost inseparable chums for some weeks, and then the kitten disappeared. The child cried and hunted among garbage cans, junk baskets, and ash heaps in the alley and up and down the street, but to no avail. When the child had grieved so much that she became ill, her grandmother went downtown to a pet shop and purchased a beautiful, aristocratic Persian kitten with glossy fur and disdainful, sophisticated cat manners, brought it home, and proudly presented the lovely creature to the little girl. But the child was not comforted. The grandmother chided the youngster, saying that she was behaving in an ungrateful and unreasonable manner. She reminded the girl that the other kitten was but a common alley cat with no good breeding and not nearly so beautiful as the feline Persian. But the child could not follow that line of adult reasoning and, between sobs, burst out with, "But Grandma! It's the inside of a cat that counts!"

Of course it is! And it's the inside of a child, and the inside of a man, and the inside of a civilization that counts, too. And life's chief perennial pleasure is in making the most of the essentials, in growing a bigger mind, in enlarging the soul, and in adding to the spiritual content of one's time. For such a satisfaction every season is a growing season.

40

Some Thoughts About Memory on an Autumn Evening

For some reason these crisp autumn evenings remind me of bonfires spouting white smoke against the night and of old men spinning rough yarns of early days of hardship and adventure. The reminiscent spirit that roams on fall nights may be conjured up by all the tokens of days past lying now around us. There are the fallen leaves, tinted memories of a verdure now rapidly fading. There are the withering grasses that but a few short months ago were on the gain, growing from tender, spindly shoots into a tall, thick lushness. In autumn most birds' songs are but thin, straggling reminders of their full summer voices. Trees, with mighty effort, can preserve only the faintest semblance of modesty as their gay garb falls from their thin shoulders. The locust is scratching his last tune, a hesitant and faint memento of gayer melodies played some weeks ago. So all over the Northland now careless Autumn, like a thoughtless picnicker, drops scraps and leavings of a finished summer.

In such a season it is natural and good to give some thought to the past. And there is nothing more conducive to the revival of mellow memories than an autumn night beside a blazing fire in the company of seasoned old veterans of life's rough-and-tumble who know how to mix history with imagination and serve it up appetizingly.

I well remember from my boyhood hearing menfolks tell of pioneering days in Michigan's Sanilac County, where my Grandfather Kohn settled upon arriving from Germany with his wife and one child, and where eleven more children were born and raised. There was the morning, for instance, when my father, then a lad not yet in his teens, was confronted by a

171

great tawny bobcat in the cow stable when he went to the barn to do the chores. Again, I recall hearing of the cringing terror of the little brood of Kohns when a spooky howling persisted outside their cabin, and they could not identify its source until someone noticed an open bottle sitting on a stump and assured the rest of the youngsters that the tuneless, weird wailing was but a prankish wind blowing across the bottle's mouth. There were also the hunting stories of how the older boys of the family coaxed the younger ones into serving as hunting dogs, tracking game on cold winter days and chasing it into openings in the woods where the hunters could get a clean shot.

I've wondered while hearing old people reminisce why, out of the thousands of experiences they have had, certain events were much more memorable than others. Why did Allie remember this hunting incident but not the other ones? Why did the aged Mr. Bates recall one near-accident in the logging woods but forget about dozens of others just as hair-raising? Why did old George remember all the details of young Henry's shellacking him in a shrewd business deal many years before and yet could not recall the name of an associate who had befriended George only a few months previously? Why do some people remember another's faults more easily than his virtues?

Of this much I am sure: there are reasons why we remember and why we forget, just as there is a reason for everything else in God's world. And if one event or name or face makes an indelible impression upon us and another is easily forgotten, it is because one has more significance to us than does another. Memory is commonly thought to be the impression the past leaves upon us. But it isn't simply that. Memory treasures what is most meaningful to us, what has evoked our highest hopes, what has instilled our deepest fears, or what has hurt us most painfully. The strangers whose names we remember best are apt to be those who have insulted us and those who have praised us, because insults and praise both affect our egos and therefore have profound significance for us. We may remember a person's faults and forget his virtues because his faults make us feel superior to him while his virtues make us feel uncomfortably inferior. We are prone to remember what most hurts or satisfies our egos.

Dr. Bruno Furst, the famed expert on memory training, once told of a fashionable woman acquaintance of his who had a disturbing experience on her way to a speaking engagement at a business function. She forgot the name of the hotel where the meeting was held, and by the time she found the place she was extremely late for the engagement. She forgot the name of the chairman of the meeting and the names of other prominent people present, and when she arose to speak she found she had forgotten what she was going to say.

When she related her frightful experience to Dr. Furst, he asked her what she had worn to the meeting. She unhesitatingly replied, "My navy silk-shantung suit, my white straw hat, my navy leather bag and shoes to match." Her stylish appearance meant most to her. She remembered that.

Many professionals, such as professors, doctors, ministers, and scientists are notoriously absent-minded. This may be because their attentions are so absorbed in remembering things that spell success in their life's work that other matters are easily overlooked and forgotten. Thomas Alva Edison was such a person, his thoughts being so preoccupied with inventions and improvements that other affairs were often neglected. One afternoon Edison got off a train at Orange, New Jersey, congratulating himself that for once he had forgotten nothing. He had checked his baggage. It was all there. He had his hat and coat and all his other belongings. For once he had remembered everything. Thomas Edison picked up his bags and started down the platform. The ticket agent, an old acquaintance of Edison's, met him and asked, "You're sure you have everything, Mr. Edison? Didn't leave anything on the train?"

Mr. Edison smiled and confidently replied, "Not this time!" Then, looking back toward the train, Edison gasped, dropped his baggage and raced for the passenger car he had just left. For at the window he saw the puzzled face of his bride of two weeks!

While forgetting one's wife cannot be recommended, Mr. Edison's kind of intense preoccupation with his life's purposes offers a lesson worth emulating. The noted inventor, like great people of all time, was so dedicated to a worth-while object that he became absent-minded about a multitude of other things. We could all afford some such dedication. If the overly sensitive person had it, he would be so absorbed in a worthy purpose that he would not notice some slights and unkind criticisms that come his way, and those that he did notice he could soon forget. Every mind and every memory is limited. The bigger the aims that fill it, the less room there is for such trash as little indignities and carping criticisms. Abraham Lincoln once explained why he could be almost absent-minded about the slurs of his political foes: "I do the best I know how, the very best I can. I mean to keep on doing this down to the very end. If the end brings me out all wrong, then ten angels swearing I had done right would make no difference. If the end brings me out all right, then what is said against me now will not amount to anything." Lincoln's mind was so full of exalted purposes that there was no space left for memories of unpleasant things said about him.

One more value of memory occurs to me. Memory attaches us securely to the future. When our time here is done, the years will not move on like a departing train, without us, leaving us lost and lone in the past. We live on, not only in some other realm, but here on earth in the memories and affections of those we leave behind. Memory makes that possible. In Springfield, Illinois, Abraham Lincoln's home is preserved, with the stoves and fireplaces, furniture and utensils he used all in place. Thousands of people pass through this Lincoln museum each year. One late evening a lady tourist and her little daughter passed the Lincoln home, and the child noticed a light glowing through the window. She exclaimed to her mother, "When Mr. Lincoln went away he left his light burning, didn't he?" Of course he did. All good people leave a light burning when they go away, burning in someone's heart, in someone's memory. And that is one of the gifts of memory: it keeps the good that is in us alive in the world long after we are gone.

41

Do You Know What You're Doing?

The elfin, winged acrobat flitting in ghostly silence from tree to tree and crawling about upside down or right-side up with equal ease is seeking its favorite food — insects, insect larvae, pupae, and eggs. He searches for them up and down the maples and the ashes. He hunts amidst the torn fibers of broken birch branches. His sharp, inquisitive beak explores the bark of spruce and hemlock, balsam and white pine. The red-breasted nuthatch, his almost insatiable craw plaguing him with a rankling hunger, investigates every tree nook and cranny, pulling from their hiding places insects in all stages of development, from egg to adult.

If the nuthatch ever ponders upon the meaning of his almost ceaseless search for insects, it must be a most primitive sort of thinking based upon a rudimentary kind of awareness. His brain is small, hardly larger than an average-size kidney bean, with a multitude of duties other than thinking, leaving little room for cogitative functions. Likely there's a hunger-consciousness somewhat akin to a half-grown boy's that prompts a nuthatch to seek a grub much as a youngster probes about in a cookie jar. But when a perky nuthatch lights on the bole of a Hidden Brook tree, he has no idea of the far-flung consequences of his insect meal.

Whenever this feathery bundle of energy sets upon a quest for insect food, he affects to some degree the entire future of the woods. He pulls bark beetles from their lairs, snatches scale insects from their banqueting, dines upon the eggs of gypsy moths, and effectively depletes the ranks of marauding multitudes of crawling six-legged creatures of all kinds. At first thought, one lone nuthatch would seem to take little toll upon the vast forest insect population. But every bird and beast that eats one destructive insect pest does the future forest immeasurable good, for every winged adult, crawling larva, or immobile egg is the potential forebear of millions of other blighters of arboreal beauty and wasters of valuable forest resources. A female beetle, producing only fifty eggs in a lifetime, could conceivably become the ancestor of 1,950 trillion beetles in the tenth generation if all its descendants were allowed to reach maturity and reproduce. A foremost authority on insect life, Dr. Lee Strong of the United States Bureau of Entomology, has said that if a single pair of aphids were to reproduce undisturbedly and their descendants were allowed to do likewise, they could in one year fill the Atlantic Ocean with offspring. Thank heaven, they are disturbed, by insect eaters and insect diseases!

When a nuthatch feasts on insects he may know a little of what he is doing, but not *all!* Besides appeasing his hunger, he is assisting trees in their constant struggle for survival against a perpetual invasion of hordes of insect enemies. He is preserving leafy shade over watery trout dens in the brook, shade without which the stream would warm under the summer sun and trout would flee to cooler waters. The saucy wee nuthatch is protecting future timber resources and scores of by-products of the lumber industries, and when he flits from the brook bank to feed on nearby apple trees, he becomes guardian of fruit crops belonging to generations yet to come. Does the nuthatch know what he's doing? Hardly. He seems only to be eating, but far beyond that he is performing an excellent and vital task of forest management.

An ancient whitetail buck seeks the warmth of sunshine and the comfort of warm mud wallows because they feel good. He doesn't know that they have a beneficial effect upon his rheumatic old body. He is doing more for himself than he knows. Almost every furred creature in the woods and fields licks its wounds, not knowing the good, aseptic effect of this action, really a sort of primitive self-doctoring. Earthworms eating their way through the soil have no awareness that their churning of the soil, bringing the subsoil to the surface and taking humus down below, enriches the good earth, nor that their worm-holes aerate the soil. They don't know what they are doing.

The American Indians used to cover wounds with balsam

gum, forming what they called a "new skin" with it. Balsam gum soothed the wound. But it did something else of greater value. The gum protected cuts against the entrance of germs, although the Indians knew nothing about the existence of germs. Their primitive medicine did more for them than they knew.

Nobody knows what he is doing—nuthatch, whitetail buck, wounded creatures of woods and meadows, earthworms, or man. We are doing more than we know.

See, first, the less pleasant implications of the premise. The evil consequences of our negligence are greater than we know. The famed medical missionary to Labrador, Dr. Grenfell, was once given a motorboat by his many friends, so that he could visit more sick people on the islands off the Labrador coast. Soon after the boat was delivered, Dr. Grenfell received an urgent call to rush to the aid of a critically ill woman on an off-shore island. The call came on a foggy night. But the great doctor and his crew, confident that the fine compass on the new boat would guide them to their destination, decided to make the voyage. The boat ended up that night far off course, amidst the rocks on the most perilous section of the coast, and the woman died without help. Why? What happened? The compass was inaccurate. It was later discovered that a lad in the Liverpool shipyards where the boat was built, in screwing the compass to its base used a steel screw when he couldn't find enough brass screws handy. It was against orders, but just one steel screw shouldn't make a difference. It did. It magnetized and deflected the compass needle so that it didn't point true. The shipyard worker thought he was only substituting a steel screw for a brass one. But he didn't know what he was doing. He was letting a woman die and endangering the lives of a ship's crew and one of the world's most heroic doctors.

When that word of warning has been considered, then turn to the more positive inference. The far-flung results of our *best* behavior are more consequential than anything we can ever guess. Tom and Nancy Lincoln nurtured a small boy of homely face and of no apparent promise. Later, when Nancy died, a step-mother took over the duties of caring for Abe and the rest of the family. They thought they were merely feeding another mouth and clothing another back, but they were providing America with a future President and influencing the history of the world. They didn't know what they were doing.

A child is given little tasks to perform, such as carrying in kindling and fireplace wood, weeding a garden, baby-sitting, or attending to the small business of a newspaper route. He thinks he is only obeying and helping his parents or earning small change. But he is learning to handle the big responsibilities of adult life by performing little chores. He is building capacities and character, although he is not aware of it.

Many a momentous and far-reaching decision hinges upon the balloting of a person who thinks his vote doesn't count for much.

Whenever parents express a spontaneous and honest affection for each other in the presence of their children they are unconsciously teaching the next generation something vital about marriage, and their happiness makes marriage attractive.

A well-timed word of encouragement, lightly given, has unwittingly saved many a person from suicide. (One depressed person I know of was spared from self-inflicted death by the impulsive affectionate nuzzling, licking, and joyful bounding of a stray dog.)

While illustrating the involved relationships of everything in this universe to all other things, Sir James Jeans, eminent British scientist, once said that an infant cannot throw its toys from its carriage without influencing the farthest star. Every action by every person on God's earth has consequences beyond the farthest stretch of imagination.

Like a red-breasted nuthatch, aware only that it is hunting insects but in the very act saving a forest, none of us knows what he is doing. That is part of the glory and wonder of life.

42

Where Does the Time Go?

It is nine o'clock on a June night and darkness descends heavily upon haze-shrouded Lake Charlevoix. Across the bay bleary lights twinkle vaguely through the low-lying mist. Messages the breezes idly scribbled across the lake's surface can now hardly be read. Light fades. Rapidly now all details of the lakeside scene are erased by the darkness, and only bold outlines and silhouettes remain.

From the tip-top twig of our brush pile a song sparrow has bid goodnight with a cheerful lullaby, and no more has been heard from him for a quarter of an hour. Now a robin chants a dreamy song from the wood's edge before retiring. Then all is still.

Another day is done. Since last night at this time the earth has made a complete turn on its axis. You have travelled twenty-five thousand miles at the dizzy speed of more than one thousand miles an hour. So have I, and so have all the earth's creatures. During those hours, say the astronomers, the earth has lost about ninety pounds of its weight, and the sun now weighs three hundred and sixty billion tons less than it did last night at this hour. You are not quite the same person you were a few hours ago. Some of your body tissues have worn out and they are being quietly replaced by an unceasing physiological process that goes on in all animal life. Every day and every hour we live in a new world, a changed world.

What is this thing we call time, that seems to change all things it touches as if it were a fairy's magic wand? Some scientists claim that time is one of the dimensions of space. If we want to determine the volume of yonder hill across the bay with a high degree of scientific accuracy, it is not enough to know the customary three dimensions, length, width, and height. Another measurement is needed which may be repre-

181

sented by the coined expression "whenth," denoting the year, day, and hour when the measurements were taken. The "whenth" measurement is required because of the unceasing alteration of all objects in this changeful universe.

A hundred thousand years ago the hill was much bulkier than it now is. When another hundred thousand or a half-million years pass, the hill may be only a small mound of dust.

As nightfall set me to musing about the constant flow of time and the ceaseless changes it brings, it occurred to me that in the gift of time we have one of life's rare equalities. We creatures of earth are not equal in all things, in intelligence, in natural gifts, abilities, skills, in appearance, in span of life. But at one point we are all equal: everyone has the same size minutes, days, weeks, and years.

Some people complain they cannot render needed service to their community or club or church because they don't have enough time. "Let someone do it who has more time than I do," they plead. But, really, no one has more time than they do. Is there anyone who has more than sixty seconds to his minutes, or more than sixty minutes to each hour? Are some people limited to only seven-hour days while others are favored with thirty-six hours or forty-eight hours in each day's span? Clearly, no one has "more time" than another in his day or week. The difference is not in the amount of time, but in how we use it.

Give each of three people a suitcase of an identical size, and give to each person a large heap of clothing and miscellaneous articles that ordinarily are carried when traveling. Then watch them pack their suitcases. One will succeed in filling his case with far more articles than the others.

Our days are like identical suitcases distributed to us by the Creator for use in our journey through life. Our days are of the same size. No one has less than twenty-four hours in each day. No one has more. Everyone's hour is sixty minutes long. A king's hour is no longer than his servant's and a President's day is the same size as a street-sweeper's. But what a difference in the way we pack our days! Methuselah lived to be nine hundred and sixty-nine years of age, and the Bible sums up all he accomplished in a few words, "And Methuselah lived an hundred eighty and seven years, and begat Lamech. And Methuselah lived after he begat Lamech seven hundred eighty and two years, and begat sons and daughters: and all the days of Methuselah were nine hundred sixty and nine years: and he died." What a record! Almost a thousand years of existence, but doing nothing with it excepting reproducing his kind!

Then again there was One who lived only thirty-three years but of whom Saint John said, as he closed his book detailing His deeds and delineating His character, "And there are also many other things which Jesus did, the which, if they could be written every one, I suppose that even the world itself could not contain the books that should be written."

Much has been made of the elusiveness of time. A short time ago I read a statement by one of my favorite authors in the field of religion in which he said, "We cannot save time in the sense we can save money or food. We can save money or food in order to have them tomorrow. There is no hoarding of time. When it is gone, it is gone forever."

I wonder. Is it really gone, lost, or is it transformed as a caterpillar is changed into a butterfly, being the same life but finding a new expression? What is this house in which we live but the mason's time, the plumber's time, the carpenter's time, and the time it took for trees to grow into lumber, and the axeman's time to cut it, the trucker's time to haul it, the wholesaler's time to handle it, and the retailer's time to sell it? We live in a house that is time, metamorphosed into shelter.

What are the gifts you give but small pieces of your life spent in making money which in turn was spent for buying gifts? All gifts are essentially contributions of time.

When one little girl heard her haste-ridden mother exclaim, "Where does the time go?" she replied, "Why, Mother, the time goes into all the things you do."

So it does. The way to make time last is to invest it in things that have abiding value.

184

43

Who's in Charge Here?

Not all of nature is beautiful and peaceful. Even a casual observer knows enough of nature's raw wildness to trouble him and to give him serious second thoughts as to whether the natural world really affords the serenity about which poets so glibly preach.

As fall moves toward winter the great muskallonge, the biggest member of the pike family of fishes, feeds voraciously as he fattens himself against the oncoming lean winter months. Floating slowly, silently as a shadow among aquatic plants along the shore, he skulks into a school of minnows or young perch or smelt and strikes savagely. The lives of small fishes are snuffed out to satisfy the hunger of a bigger fish, and minnows, perch, or smelt are transformed into muskallonge flesh.

This is the way it is with nature. This is the way it has been from the beginning and will be to the end of time. Life subsists by feeding upon other life. A perch is eaten by a musky and becomes musky tissue. Grass is consumed by snowshoe hare and becomes hare flesh, and in its turn snowshoe hare is eaten by red fox and by nature's miracle becomes fox protoplasm. Grain is devoured by a ring-neck pheasant. The pheasant is shot down and eaten by a sportsman and his family and pheasant is transformed into human flesh. Every hour of the day and night something is dying that something else might live. Sacrifice is at the very heart of nature.

This natural scheme of keeping life going by causing all organisms to be nourished by other life has been upsetting to many a thinker. Some see it as nature's ruthlessness. Some think of it as cruelty, indifference to pain, or wastefulness.

But a person familiar with nature knows that amidst wild creatures the evil of pain is seldom present, and nothing is ultimately wasted. The rapidity of killing among predators is

miraculously fast and merciful. A young perch knows no death throes. Its seizure is affected swiftly. The musky does not tantalize it, but simply engulfs it. The killing of a mouse by a rattlesnake has been timed at a mere thirteen seconds. A robin slain by a hawk dies sooner. Even among the higher animals there is surprisingly less pain at the moment death threatens than one would expect. Dr. David Livingstone, after being attacked by a lion, testified that he sensed no pain while held by the lion's jaws.

In the strictest sense, cruelty means enjoyment in inflicting unnecessary pain. There is almost no cruelty in wild nature. Man seems to possess a monopoly on such meanness. Even a cat playing with a mouse is not aware of inflicting anguish upon his prey.

And as to wastefulness in nature, there is none. Alive or dead, everything is a part of the entire Scheme of Things. Everything has a place and while alive plays one role and when dead plays another, but nothing is wasted. Still, with conscious cruelty and wastefulness ruled out, there is enough trouble on the earth to give any thinker serious pause.

The presence of suffering and death in our world can seldom be satisfactorily explained to one who is feeling their onslaught, but we can be certain there is some reason for them if the Creator is intelligent and loving, which are minimal Christian beliefs.

On a number of occasions I have visited the shops of plumbers, automotive mechanics, and electrical repairmen. In each place I have seen instruments foreign to my own experience and beyond my immediate comprehension. But how foolish I would have been had I urged the craftsmen to discard their instruments because, as far as I could see, they were useless! Or had I picked up a tool and cut myself on it, not understanding its use or operation, how stupid to accuse the shopkeeper of cruelty or indifference to my welfare because he had not stopped my idle tampering, or because he had not prevented my entering his hazard-filled workshop.

This world is God's workshop where He is planning and creating, with wisdom and skill that far exceed our own, and with tools that we do not, as yet, understand. But the tools include struggle and pain and the experience we call death.

While we are here we might well try to understand their purposes and uses. But when understanding reaches its limits, I shall not blame the Craftsman for owning equipment I am not wise enough to comprehend, nor find fault because I sometimes get hurt, nor criticize the hospitality of One who has allowed me into His place of business.

When we have big business to transact, we do not want to deal with clerks or floor-sweepers, doormen or handymen, or even departmental foremen. We want to see the person in charge of the company, the general manager. So when we appear at the establishment for a business dealing, our first question is apt to be, "Who's in charge here?"

As we look out upon our world at the beginning of every day, that is a question well worth asking, "Who's in charge here?" Is the Power controlling this universe capable of handling His job? Does He know what He is doing? Is He so slipshod that certain departments are badly mishandled or overlooked? What about the Testing and Suffering Departments? How about the Death Division? And the Bureau of Ultimate Justice? And especially, does He have a firm hand on the Office of Future Developments? The sensible answer to such questions is that a Power wise enough and imaginative enough to create this kind of universe is wise enough, imaginative enough, and mighty enough to control it, now and forever. Sound sense can lead to a strong faith.

One of the great teachers in the history of Boston University was Professor Borden P. Bowne. He was a philosopher whose profound knowledge of history and penetrating insight into human nature kept him from radical optimism. Yet he was a person of quiet faith in the future. Bowne had a learned friend, Professor McCabe, who did not share Dr. Bowne's expectation that the universe would be safe in the capable grasp of the Almighty. One night while on a trip Dr. Bowne stopped off in Delaware to see his friend McCabe. After the customary greeting of old acquaintances, the two scholars began to debate on the existence and nature of God, and the lively discussion did not end until three o'clock in the morning. When Bowne took his leave in the morning, McCabe shouted after him as he passed through the gate, "Bowne, do you think God would have created this world if He had seen how it was coming out?" And

Bowne called back, "McCabe, do you think God would have created this world if He hadn't seen how it was coming out?"

It is incomprehensible that a wise God would have started something so tremendous as this universe with no plan for how it would be completed. It is still more incredible that the Creator would expend His thoughts and His loving care upon such a world as this and then carelessly leave it unprotected, to be destroyed by the foolishness or wantonness of men.

When James Russell Lowell was fifty years of age and had seen much of man's foolishness as well as his goodness, he said, "I take great comfort in God. I think He is considerably amused with us sometimes, but that He likes us, on the whole, and would not let us get at the match box so carelessly as He does, unless He knew that the frame of His universe was fireproof."

The General Manager in charge of Universal Operations, Incorporated, knows and controls what is going on in His many departments, including the Office of Future Developments.

44

Going Home

Springtime is home-going time in nature.

Now migrating birds return to their Northwoods nesting sites, and soon we shall hear the poignant evening song of the wood thrush, its bell-tones ringing rich and full and free through the birches and conifers as the half-light after sundown fades and darkness settles over our greening woodlands. A wood thrush nest will be built not far from Hideaway House as was done last year and the year before and likely for centuries before a cabin graced the brook bank at Wood's Creek. But now that man has invaded this quiet sanctuary, new construction materials, not used in the yesterdays, may be borrowed from our premises for properly equipping a wood thrush home with a modern accent. These birds have been known to use pop straws in their nest-building. But whatever supplies the thrushes collect, they will fashion their nests here on this acreage which they regard as home and to which they return each spring from their wintering quarters in Central America.

One day last week I walked along the trail leading to the Upper Falls on Tahquamenon River in Michigan's Upper Peninsula. The tourist season had not yet begun, and I was all alone as I approached the spectacular cataract. Suddenly the air was rent with the shrill pipings of hundreds of migrating warblers, chirping, calling, and singing excitedly. Then I saw them, darting from the towering hemlocks to little pools for a quick drink of melted snow, then swooping up to the tree tops again. I was walking through a caravan of home-going birds.

What the old Norsemen called "heimgang," home-going, prevails now in nature. Some fishes that winter in deep waters of big lakes or great oceans, but prefer the shallows for home-making, now return to ponds and streams.

While most of our northern butterflies spend their winters

right here in deep sleep, either as eggs or pupae or adults, the big red-brown monarch butterflies with black-veined wings are migrators. Last fall they gathered in huge flocks and drifted hundreds of miles southward. Soon, now, they will come home.

Insects and spiders that summer in hedges and shrubs but descend into the ground-cover of leaf-mould for the winter, now emerge and clamber about again on leaves and twigs where they are more at home.

So it will be, bob-o-links will arrive from Argentina, barn swallows from Brazil, yellow warblers from Yucatan, wood thrushes from Central America, insects, reptiles, amphibia, and all the rest from their winter hiding places. They will all come home.

The experience of death, it seems to me, is the springtime of the soul when all spirits go homeward, toward where they belong, the evil and the good alike moving toward their own kind and their own place.

A student of moral philosophy once asked Mark Hopkins, President Garfield's boyhood teacher, who would be in heaven, and he replied that he did not know, but that he was positive that no one would be in heaven who did not feel at home there. That kind of sound thinking complies with the universal law that we are drawn toward the things to which our hearts belong. The materialist would not feel at home in heaven since there would be no money there for him to jingle and no material prizes he could fondle. The hate-monger would be ill at ease and stifled there because the atmosphere is that of love. Those who live godlessly here would feel strange there as guests in God's house. But all who live by eternal things here, who have colonized the earth with a touch of heaven and whose friendship with God has been intimate and growing — they will feel at home.

For the heavenly, death is only a spring migration, going home.

45

Unknown and Known

Whenever we visit Hidden Brook these days we hear the sharp call of scarlet tanagers which each year make their homes somewhere near Hideaway House. The male, a flaming torch of feathers, can occasionally be seen hopping about in the tall white birches while the seclusive and somber female tends her nesting chores somewhere amidst concealing leaves. But more often we hear the male's loud "zzzrrheet, zzzrreet; zzheeu, zzheuu" without catching a glimpse of him. The scarlet tanager has unusual gifts of ventriloquism, and his jolly caroling draws us toward a certain cedar copse or birch clump when the bird himself is a hundred yards away in another direction. Then when early fall arrives we shall see no tanagers at all. They disappear.

Not many years ago North Americans were mystified about where scarlet tanagers went in the winter time. But now we know. After they have raised their families of four or five young high up in the crowns of trees where thick foliage protects them against the prying eyes of their enemies, the male loses his brilliant dress of red and black and, hardly distinguishable from his yellowish green and dusky gray mate, in this traveling suit the male and his mate fly to the tropics — Central America and South America — where they spend the winter stuffing themselves on insects and getting ready for another summer in the North.

Our family of scarlet tanager neighbors at Hidden Brook sometimes reminds me of the strange mixture of knowns and unknowns with which we are compelled to have dealings in this life. Tanager calls tell us the birds are near us, but because of their ventriloquist skills we do not always know how near or in which direction. We know tanagers have nests and raise young at Hidden Brook, for the male's song is a joyous proclamation of squatter's rights and a paeon of praise for family life. But the nests themselves are so well concealed that their

location is seldom known. We are aware, too, that the female who is now feeding her brood insects that pervade every yard of our woodland, will wear pretty much the same somber garb all year around while the male changes clothing at least twice each year, alternating between glowing scarlet, accented with black, and a drab suit of greenish gray. But how is the change in the male affected? What chemical transformation within the bird triggers the outer change?

And when tanagers head southward, what compass guides their certain flight to a pin-point spot in far-off Central or South America? We know much about our tanager neighbors, but the unknown by far exceeds the known.

So it is with all of nature, our ignorance always exceeds our knowledge. It was not until 1925 that the life history of eels was known, how the common eels of our streams and ponds migrate to the seas and to somewhere just north of the West Indies and there breed and die. Then, later, the baby eels come migrating across the mighty tossing waters and to the streams of their ancestors. That much has been known since the 1920's, but what is unknown is greater still. What is that strange force that guides a baby eel back to the old homestead his ancestors knew but which he has never seen?

Who knows a definite, clear, and final answer to the mystery of electricity? Even the physicists claim they have not yet fathomed the riddle of what electricity *is*, although they know what it *does*. But we know how to flick a switch and get electric light, or turn a knob and obtain electric power.

The best way of handling the unknown is not to be terrified or depressed by our ignorance, our doubts, and life's yawning mysteries, but to do something with what little we do know. Thomas Edison professed an abysmal ignorance. He said that we don't know the millionth part of one per cent about anything. Yet Edison translated the known millionth part of one per cent into history-making inventions.

Ignorance and doubt are alike in this: while all of us have a measure of them, neither is enough to live by. Edison's ignorance of the mysterious could not keep him from experimenting with what little he knew. He lived by the known. While it is often necessary to entertain doubt, we cannot successfully live by our unbeliefs. Columbus doubted the old geographical conceptions of his day — that the earth is flat and that the Atlantic ended suddenly out beyond the horizon, dropping off into a horror-filled abyss inhabited by dragons. But while Columbus disbelieved the old geography, he was not content to be doubtful. While negatively doubting the old geography, he positively believed in a round earth. He had faith there were other lands out beyond the horizon. Columbus was badly mistaken about some of the things he believed. As someone has said of him, "When Columbus sailed from Europe, he did not know where he was going. When he touched yonder shore, he did not know where he was. When he returned from America, he did not know where he had been. Still, he discovered America." Columbus doubted that there was only the earth's edge out there, an abyss and dragons, and he had contemporaries who shared these doubts with him. What made Christopher Columbus greater than the rest was his faith. He lived by faith. Driven by a compulsive faith, and in spite of all his mistakes, Columbus won a new world through faith.

Well, as for me, a long time ago I made up my mind that what I don't know is vast in extent, but what I do know has immense significance to me and is enough to live by.

There are moments when I would find it hard to say what I believe, but I always know Whom I believe.

There are numerous mysteries about which I must confess "I do not know," but concerning everything I have the faith that "it is known."

Usually I do not know the meaning of trouble or its exact purpose, but, thank God, I do know *it has a meaning* and a purpose. And while I know not why trouble comes, I do know that once it arrives it can be put to work helping me build a character.

I can know very little about God, but I can know God.

I know not what the future holds, but I know Who holds the future.

Life would be uninteresting and boring in a universe that could be completely understood, and a full and abundant life would be impossible if there were no understanding at all. The balanced life is lived by one who stands rapt in awe and reverence at the unknown while living true to the highest that he knows.